YOUR SPIRITUAL JOURNEY

to
God's Planned Destination

Ed Dittrich

Foreword by Malcolm B. Yarnell III

Editing by Lisa Bell

Book design by Radical Women

ISBN: 978-0-578-81433-9

This book is dedicated to my Lord Jesus Christ and all who long for his ultimate purpose to be fulfilled in their lives.

Contents

Acknowledgments

I want to express my heartfelt gratitude to people who made significant contributions to the writing of this book.

- To my lovely wife, Louise, of 60 plus years, who patiently served as a sounding board for theological thought and wording choices, and who was my basic grammar and spelling checker.
- To my oldest son, David, who continually encouraged me to boldly proclaim biblical truth as I understand it, regardless of tradition and conflicting viewpoints.
- To my youngest son, Mark, who forced me, through rigorous and unrelenting philosophic persuasion, to clearly identify my intended reader, to unambiguously say what I truly believe, and to be logically consistent in my message.
- To my daughter, Cindi, who took valuable time from her varied and complex professional commitments to suggest editorial changes that greatly enhanced the book's readability.
- To Dr. Malcolm Yarnell (Research Professor of Systematic Theology at Southwestern Seminary) who took valuable time from his vocation/ministry to vet the book's theological content and graciously write its Foreword.

Most of all, I am eternally grateful to God (Father, Son, and Holy Spirit) for graciously gifting me with the evangelistic aptitude and passion to write the book. My heart's desire is that he alone will be glorified by its existence.

"But I do not account my life of any value nor as precious to myself, if only I may finish my course and the ministry that I received from the Lord Jesus, to testify to the gospel of the grace of God."
~Acts 20:24, ESV

Authenticity and Grace
A Foreword

Many Christians set out to share their faith in the good news about Jesus Christ with friends, family, and strangers. A few have taken the tremendous effort to do so in writing. Sometimes, these oral or written efforts are a mixture of truth and self-service. However, in the case of Ed Dittrich, you have the unique opportunity to hear from the heart of a man indelibly marked by authenticity and grace. He truly is, as Jesus said of Nathanael, a man "in whom is no guile."

In my own walk with the Lord and among his people as a Pastor and as a Theologian, I have encountered Christians at every level of maturity. Please trust me when I tell you that this man is among the most mature, humble, and loving I have ever encountered. He is authentic about his own limits and his failures, and he is emphatic that God truly does extend grace to those who understand how needy they really are.

Ed Dittrich is a "follower of Jesus Christ," and he wants to introduce you to the Master who has blessed him with forgiveness, life, and joy. Through a combination of apologetics, of story, of Bible study, and of praise toward God, Ed seeks to bless you. He is willing to open his life up to you and thereby to show you how the Word of God applies to everything that matters.

This book is intended both for unbelievers and for believers. If you will take a moment to hear him, you will be quickly drawn into and fascinated by a life marked with authenticity and by the God who made him this way. You will also develop a desire to know as much as possible about this God, this Jesus, this Holy Spirit who offers you the grace you need to follow Jesus into eternity. May you desire to follow Ed as he follows Jesus.

Malcolm B. Yarnell III
Research Professor, Systematic Theology, Southwestern Seminary
Teaching Pastor, Lakeside Baptist Church
Author of *God the Trinity* and *The Formation of Christian Doctrine*

Introduction

I am writing this book in my 80th year. It is my first and likely only book. I have no qualifications for writing it other than being a follower and maturing servant of the Lord Jesus for over forty years. During this time, I have fulfilled my calling (gifting) within the body of Christ as a non-vocational evangelist. In this capacity, I have seen thousands of people, in many countries of the world, embark on new spiritual journeys. However, looking back, I am now deeply concerned that my messages, up until the past several years, failed to provide sufficient directions for a successful journey.

I am concerned because that is what happened to me and similarly to many others I know and associate with. I started a spiritual journey at age 12, based on somewhat sketchy and incoherent directions. I then wandered in a spiritual wilderness for twenty-five years before realizing I wasn't on a journey to God's planned destination. It was only through God's gracious intervention that I was given the opportunity to begin anew. The ensuing journey has far exceeded anything I could have imagined. (If you are interested in details about this journey, you can turn to Appendix 1 before reading the rest of the book.) As a result, I have a deep-seated desire for other people to experience a similar journey. Thus, the impetus for this book!

Although my hope and prayer are that any honest truth seekers would read and seriously consider the message of the book, it is written primarily to those who self-identify as Christians and reside in the U.S. Your common denominator is that you can point to circumstances and a moment in time that initiated the spiritual journey you are currently traveling. You may have responded to a gospel presentation in a church service or at an evangelistic event, said a "sinner's prayer" during a personal witnessing or media presentation, or successfully completed some church confirmation process. However, regardless of the circumstances, you believe you have done everything that is necessary to secure a place in Heaven when your time on Earth is complete.

Since you are a professing Christian, I assume you believe that the Bible is the inspired and infallible Word of God and thereby the only source of absolute truth. Everything I share in the book is based on this assumption. If you have any questions or doubts about the Bible as a credible roadmap for a spiritual journey, please turn to Appendix 2 before reading the rest of the book. If your doubts are caused by "apparent" conflicts between modern science and biblical claims, you may find Appendix 3 helpful.

My objective for the book is to help you, as a professing Christian, experience all that God has planned for you during your time on planet Earth and in eternity. Jesus said, "I came that they might have life and have it abundantly." (John 10:10) The abundant life he described can start now, while we are on planet Earth. It provides the meaning and purpose we are innately searching for. But it can only be experienced as we travel a journey toward God's planned destination.

When I use the phrase "God's planned destination," you may immediately think "Heaven." Yes, the final physical destination for biblical Christians is Heaven. However, in this book, when I use "God's planned destination," I am referring to our current life on planet Earth.

I would like for you to ask yourself this question: "Am I currently traveling a spiritual journey that is taking me to where God wants to take me during this life?" Hopefully, this book will help you make that determination. If you determine you aren't on a journey to God's planned destination, the book provides directions for transitioning to such a journey.

As I contemplated writing the book, the many journeys my wife and I have undertaken during the past sixty-plus years came to mind. We have had the privilege of traveling to many parts of the world. However, our favorite journeys are road trips to explore remote, scenic areas within the U.S. where we reside.

In preparation for these journeys, we jointly agree on a destination. My wife then selects a roadmap from the large collection she accumulated over the years. She is the navigator, and I am the driver. As navigator, she carefully studies the waypoints that will lead to our chosen destination and provides driving directions for me. Although the waypoints are clearly marked, inevitably there will be unanticipated hazards and diversions between waypoints that have to be safely navigated.

In this book, I will perform the role of navigator for a spiritual journey that leads to God's planned destination. I will use the Bible as a roadmap with well-established waypoints to guide the way. But you will have to drive; it will be your unique journey. Your travel experiences will likely be different from mine, but if we carefully follow the roadmap, you will arrive safely at God's planned destination.

I pray this book will honor God and be useful in furthering his kingdom objectives!

Part 1
God's Planned Journey

We are not here on planet Earth by accident; we are the pinnacle of God's creation.

His plan for humanity can best be understood as a spiritual journey described in the Bible.

The first part of this book describes my concerns about the spiritual journeys many professing Christians seem to be traveling.

It then describes my understanding of the starting place and destination for a spiritual journey that must be travelled to fully experience God's plan.

Although my understanding stems from over forty years as a passionate seeker of biblical truth, a practicing evangelist in many parts of the world, and corroboration by personal experience, it's certainly not infallible.

So please be like the Bereans who "received the word with all eagerness, examining the Scriptures daily to see if these things were so." (Acts 17:11)

Chapter 1
My Concern

When I started sharing the gospel as a budding evangelist, I tended to think God's plan for humanity had various status levels - kind of like credit cards or insurance policies. The Silver Plan was to "accept Jesus as Savior," which resulted in forgiveness of sin and a free ticket to Heaven. A Gold Plan added a few "do and don't" rules, participation in church life, and maybe some involvement in Christian ministry. A Platinum Plan was reserved for those special few who became pastors or missionaries.

As an evangelist, I saw my role as helping people to adopt the Silver Plan. Once they signed up for it, they would hopefully upgrade to the Gold Plan. Maybe some would eventually even subscribe for the Platinum Plan.

However, as time went on, I saw that the contemporary evangelistic messages I and others shared were not producing results consistent with descriptions of the early church we read about in the Bible.

This observation caused great frustration and led me to begin questioning the validity of the messages. When talking to other evangelists and church leaders about my observations, I found that many shared my frustration.

I remember one particular conversation that highlighted this frustration. I had participated in an evangelistic mission project in one of the Central or South American countries. The pastor of a large church in Dallas also participated in the project. On the way back home, we had a layover in the Miami airport. During the layover, I engaged the pastor in a lunchtime conversation.

I asked, "How many people in your congregation do you think are genuine followers of Jesus?"

I will never forget his response. He looked me directly in the eyes in an angry, almost hostile way, and replied, "It's your generation's fault!"

It was time to catch our flight, so I didn't have an opportunity to explore what he was saying. But I've thought a lot about it since.

As I think back over my seventy-plus years of being exposed to contemporary gospel messages, I can see his point. Sometime before my generation came on the scene, the biblical gospel message began to get diluted. This dilution continued during my lifetime to the point where today's messages as proclaimed by many Christian leaders, evangelistic ministries, and individuals are almost "toothless." As a result, they have lost much of their power to transform, overcome, and enable as God intended.

Thus, I have a deep concern about the spiritual journey that many professing Christians are traveling. In a nutshell, my concern is that they aren't on a spiritual journey that leads to God's planned destination and, even worse, they may be wandering in a spiritual wilderness and in danger of dying there. I hurt for these people because they are missing so much, and God's kingdom suffers as a result.

As a prelude to addressing this concern, let me first describe the abundant life God designed for all who belong to him.

ABUNDANT LIFE

The Bible describes humans as much more than the product of random mating between sperm and egg cells. We are the pinnacle of God's creation! He knew each of us before he created anything. In accordance with his plan, each of us exists in a sliver of time we call life. This very limited time is the only opportunity we ever have to discover who God is and his plan for our being. If we miss this, we will miss what life is about!

Jesus was describing the life God designed for his people when he said, "I came that they may have life and have it abundantly." (John 10:10) The original Greek word translated "life" in this scripture can mean physical existence, but, in this context, it means much more. It's the kind of life God possesses. It's supernatural and eternal!

Jesus used this same Greek word when he said, "I am the way, and the truth, and the life." (John 14:6) We can only receive this life through Jesus. We receive it through new birth. (John 3:1-8) When we have this life, the Bible describes us as "a new creation." (2 Corinthians 5:17)

Jesus further explains that not only can we have this life, but we can "have it abundantly." The Greek word that translates to "abundantly" has connotations of extraordinary, surpassing, and uncommon. When I contemplate these descriptors, the picture of Niagara Falls comes to mind. Even though I heard about and saw pictures of Niagara Falls' majesty, my expectations were far exceeded when I experienced it in person.

The apostle Paul described the practical application of this life in Romans 8. It's an overcoming life, a life lived by the

Spirit, a life that is continually being conformed to the image of Jesus, a life in which all things work together for good, a secure life, and a life lived as sons and daughters of God. *It is the life that God predestined for all who belong to him!*

As I contemplate the abundant life Jesus came to give, I think about professing Christians whom I have personally known and associated with during my spiritual journey. Some of them are obviously experiencing an abundant life, but others aren't. Why is this?

In the course of answering the question, let me describe three groups of professing Christians whom I have observed over the years. They all began their spiritual journeys based on directions they received. Typically, they received these directions through some type of evangelistic messaging as children or teens, or as adults during some kind of major life transition or crisis.

Group 1

Professing Christians in this group are like I was in early adulthood. They may attend church sporadically or on special occasions, but regular participation in church life is not a priority. They think they have their ticket to heaven, and that is all the spiritually they need.

Most, based on adherence to societal or self-imposed rules, attempt to convince themselves and others that they are "good" Christian folks. Like the Pharisees of Jesus' time, they revel in this label. However, their life focus is materialistic as opposed to spiritual. Thus, they attempt to fulfill their innate need for meaning and purpose with such things as human achievements, material possessions, sports, adventures, pleasures, human relationships, etc.

Some eventually get caught in one or more of Satan's snares – such as unethical or illegal behaviors, addictions of various types, sexual immorality or perversions. When their lifestyles conflict with biblical guidelines, they sometimes attempt to justify their behavior by simply dismissing, misinterpreting, or misapplying condemning scripture passages.

If and when they pray, their prayers are typically rote and self-focused, generally based on the traditions of their childhoods or what they have otherwise been exposed to.

But, regardless of appearances or lifestyles, the reality of God's kingdom (his rule) in their lives is always subservient to "the cares of the world and the deceitfulness of riches." (Matthew 13:22) In practical effect, there is little, if any, difference between their lives and the lives of "good" non-Christians.

Group 2

Professing Christians in this group regularly attend church and are generally considered good people. I realize "good" is a relative term, and only God is truly good. That being understood, the people in this group generally have higher moral and ethical standards, more stable family relationships, more compassion, better reputations, and generally experience a better quality of life than many of their contemporaries.

Spirituality is part of but not the dominant attribute in their lives. Their primary life focus is secular. They attend church to hear sermons and may participate in Bible studies or social functions. Their doctrinal beliefs are generally based on church tradition rather than personal conviction. They typically are uncomfortable in personal or even small group discussions about spiritual topics. Their Christianity is in a very small box, and anything outside of that box is off limits.

If the subject of personal sin ever comes up, they have a defeatist attitude. They see themselves in an ongoing battle with sin they can't win. Since they hear others express the same attitude, they resign themselves to the conclusion that they are living a normal Christian life.

This group readily agrees that all Christians should be involved in good works. However, they don't typically have a sense of calling to particular good works. As a result, they may feel obligated from time to time to be involved in some kind of ministry, usually of a social welfare type. However, because their good works are driven by a sense of obligation and not by God's calling, they are susceptible to spiritual burnout. They have some concern about the spiritual status of people they know, but not to the degree that would lead them to engage in personal evangelism.

When you listen to this group's prayer concerns, they are typically clustered around crisis situations (such as health, provision, and comfort needs) in theirs or the lives of people they know. Sometimes their concerns extend to church or society related issues or catastrophic events. However, their concerns can generally be categorized as personal instead of God focused.

The end result for this group is that they eventually accept the status quo and settle into typical church life. At this point, they have become institutionalized and will seldom, if ever, venture outside their comfort zone.

Group 3

Professing Christians in this group share many of the good lifestyle characteristics of Group 2. However, their primary life focus is spiritual. Some in this group came into God's kingdom at an early age and have experienced continual spiritual growth. However, this is atypical. Most had a "Damascus Road" type experience where there was a clear departure from an old life to begin a new one. They are typically more biblically literate than other professing Christians. They are more comfortable in non-traditional church services and open Bible studies. They have formed their own opinions on most doctrinal issues. Sometimes these opinions extend beyond the boundaries of their church tradition. They flourish in personal or small group discussions of spiritual topics. Their Christianity box is much larger than Groups 1 or 2.

Although they don't claim sinless perfection, they don't view personal sin as an insurmountable issue. They understand "the law of the Spirit of life has set you free in Christ Jesus from the law of sin and death." (Romans 8:2) This means they no longer have to live as "sold under sin" as described in Romans 7:14-19, but can live free as "sons of God" as described in Romans 8:1-14. When the Holy Spirit makes them aware of a particular sin issue, they readily repent in order to remain in close fellowship with their Father. They see the normal Christian as one who "*practices righteousness*." (1 John 3:7, emphasis added) Righteousness to them is not just "positional" or "imputed," it is real and active!

This group sees themselves as God's "workmanship, created in Christ Jesus for good works." (Ephesians 2:10) As a result, they typically have a strong sense of calling to particular good works. They passionately and wholeheartedly perform the good works they believe God created them to accomplish. Their calling becomes their life's focus. They have a deep concern for the lost and naturally lead others to a personal relationship with God.

The prayer concerns of this group include all of life issues, but are generally more spiritually oriented. Their focus is God's kingdom. As a result, they regularly ask God to intervene in the lives of lost people and world events. Also, since they are very sensitive to the leading of the Holy Spirit during daily activities, they effectively "pray without ceasing." (1 Thessalonians 5:17)

If this group senses a clear leading of the Holy Spirit, they will step out of their comfort zone. In addition to normal church activities, they sometimes start personal ministries or involve themselves in parachurch organizations whose missions align with their particular calling. Because they are responding to a call as opposed to a perceived obligation, they are less prone to spiritual burnout. As a result, they experience deep personal fulfillment and an ever-increasing oneness with their Creator.

CONCLUSIONS

So, what can we conclude from the descriptions of these three groups? As stated earlier, they all started their spiritual journeys based on directions they received. However, it's obvious Groups 1 and 2 aren't experiencing the abundant life Jesus came to give, but Group 3 is, at least to a much greater degree. As asked previously, "Why is this?"

I won't pretend to definitively answer this question for all people and situations. However, it's clear that something is different about Group 3. I see two possibilities: 1) they either started on the spiritual journey God designed for them, or 2) they later transitioned to it. Based on personal experience and observations during the past forty-plus years, the latter possibility is by far the dominant case.

Thus, I conclude that most professing Christians started their spiritual journey based on faulty or incomplete directions. This happened to me, and based on testimonies across a broad spectrum of people I have known and associated with, this also happened to them.

In the following two chapters, I will provide biblically correct directions for a spiritual journey that leads to God's planned destination. These directions will provide information needed to decide whether you are already traveling that journey or need to transition to it.

If you conclude that you are not on a journey to God's planned destination, but decide to continue the journey you are on, I must issue a warning. You are in great danger! You may squeeze into heaven, but it will be "as through fire." (1 Corinthians 3:15) In that case, you and God's kingdom will suffer great loss. But more likely you will hear words from Jesus that I deeply dread for anyone, "I never knew you." (Matthew 7: 23)

Chapter 2
The Starting Place

To experience the "abundant life" God planned, we must travel a spiritual journey he designed. As is the case for all journeys, God's plan has a well-defined starting place and destination. The specific journey for each person will be unique, but the starting place, some critical waypoints, and the destination are common to all travelers. The common waypoints and other key aspects of the journey will be described in subsequent parts of the book. This chapter focuses on the starting place for a spiritual journey that leads to God's planned destination.

Several years ago, in preparation for a mission trip, I thought about New Testament terms used to describe people in the early church. Four terms came to mind: Christian, Disciple, Saint, and Servant.

When I examined the context of when and how these terms were used, the results were eye-opening. It dramatically changed the way I understand and share the gospel.

If we are going to embark on a successful spiritual journey, we need to understand and fully embrace our *biblical identities*!

NEW TESTAMENT IDENTITIES

The following information was gathered from word searches in the Bible and readily accessible online Bible study tools.

Christian

The term Christian is used a total of three times in the New Testament (twice in the book of Acts and once in 1 Peter). It is interesting to note that some biblical scholars think the term was coined by non-Christians to describe followers of Jesus. Today, especially in Western societies, the term Christian can mean almost anything. For some people, it is associated with moral and ethical conduct. For others, it is a cultural identification. Still others associate it with church attendance.

However, the **biblical definition** of a Christian can be understood from the New Testament statement, "And in Antioch the disciples were first called Christians." (Acts 11:26) Note that they *were disciples* who were *called Christians*! Therefore, the biblical definition of a Christian is simply a disciple of Jesus. As such, it will be covered in the following description for disciples, which is a well-defined term.

Disciple

The term disciple is used a total of twenty-six times in the book of Acts to describe people in the early church. On multiple occasions, it is clearly used to describe *all people who composed the early church*. (e.g. - Acts 6:1, 7; 9:1, 38; 11:26, 29; 14:20, 21, 22, 28; 15:10; 18:23, 27; 19:1; 20:1, 30; and 21:4, 16)

While contemplating this, I found one scripture reference to be particularly interesting. The apostle Paul was on a missionary trip that led to the city Derbe. I haven't been able to determine how long he stayed there, but from the context, it appears to be a short time – probably days or less. But during his time there, they "preached the gospel" and *"made many disciples."* (Acts 14:21-22, emphasis added)

The clear implication is that disciples were made when they heard the gospel preached. I see the same thing as applicable today. However, for this to happen, the *biblical gospel*, as opposed to some diluted version of it, must be faithfully proclaimed. (My understanding of the biblical gospel that must be proclaimed is described in Part 2 of the book.)

So, if people who comprised the early church became disciples when they heard the gospel message, what had they become? A disciple (biblical or not) can be simply understood as a pupil who commits to follow and thereby learn from someone whom they consider authoritative. In the New Testament church, the authoritative person was Jesus. But Jesus was no longer present on planet Earth, so they needed someone to tell them about him so they could, in effect, become one of his followers. The Bible identifies this teacher as the Holy Spirit. He primarily used the original apostles to convey truth about Jesus and his teachings and commands to those who became his followers. Today the Holy Spirit uses the Bible, which includes the original apostle's teachings, to accomplish the same objective. When we commit to live by Jesus' teachings and commands, we too are his disciples (followers of Jesus) in the same sense as the early disciples.

It is important to understand there is no connotation of spiritual maturity associated with being a disciple. This is contrary to much of contemporary Christian teaching. Most teaching I have been exposed to somehow equates discipleship with spiritual maturity. The general concept of such teaching is that a person first becomes a Christian and then sometime later, as they mature spiritually, they may become a disciple. Discipleship is thereby sometimes seen as optional.

However, this is not the picture we see in the Bible. As explained earlier, all the people in the early church started their spiritual journeys as disciples. They had limited knowledge and were spiritually immature, but they learned and matured as they followed Jesus. Sometimes they stumbled and fell. Many times, they had to be reprimanded and forgiven, but their spiritual direction never changed. They were on an intensively focused path to fulfill God's plan for their lives.

Jesus had very stringent requirements for his disciples that could result in substantial personal sacrifice. Jesus repeatedly exhorted those who expressed an interest in following him to count the costs. Many started to follow Jesus, but found the requirements too demanding and subsequently fell by the wayside. But those who persevered found the reward to be exceedingly well worth the costs. Even in the face of martyrdom, they never reversed course. Their spiritual GPS had been forever set!

Saint

The term saint is used a total of sixty times (three times in Acts and fifty-seven times in the Epistles). The term can be understood to mean one who is separated from worldly influences and consecrated to God.

It is important to realize this term doesn't only apply to a few spiritual "superstars," or to someone designated by a human institution such as the Catholic Church. It applies to *all* disciples.

Servant

The term servant is used a total of thirty-three times. Most of the New Testament Epistle authors (Paul, James, Peter, and Jude) used this term to describe themselves.

The term can be understood to mean those who are used by God to accomplish his kingdom objectives. As opposed to disciple, this definition has clear connotations of maturity. The maturity happens as a natural consequence of following Jesus. This was the case for Jesus' original disciples and equally applies today.

STUDY CONCLUSIONS

So, what can be concluded from my study?

- All who experience biblical salvation are disciples (followers) of Jesus.
- All disciples have been set apart for God's purpose.
- As disciples mature, they take on the role of servants.

Thus, the starting place for a spiritual journey that leads to

God's planned destination is to become a disciple (a follower) of Jesus!

PERSONAL NOTE

At this point I need to be very clear! Throughout this book I repeatedly use the phrases "follower of Jesus," or equivalently "Jesus-follower," to describe modern disciples. If professing Christians are asked if they are a follower of Jesus, they most likely will respond affirmatively. However, by this response, I believe many (maybe most) would be simply acknowledging that they intellectually believe in Jesus. In this book, being a follower of Jesus is much more than intellectual belief in him. It's synonymous with biblical disciples who submitted to Jesus' Lordship and were thereby subject to all his teachings and commands.

I recently heard a well-known and respected Christian leader say something to the effect of, "The call to salvation and the call to discipleship are separate callings."

I tremble when I say this, but based on everything I have come to believe about biblical Christianity, I have to respectfully disagree. I believe that leader's statement summarizes a diluted gospel message that caused problems in my spiritual journey and is the root cause of many problems we observe in contemporary Christianity, especially within the U.S.

As mentioned in the Introduction, I experienced a life-changing encounter with God at age 37. That day my life was dramatically transformed. I was immediately set free from several sin strongholds I had struggled with for years. As I fed my new spiritual appetite from biblical studies, sermons, teachings, books, articles, etc., I developed an intense desire to begin fulfilling the purpose I had been created for.

However, for many years, I didn't understand, nor was I able to explain what happened to me. As a result of new insight gained from the above study, I finally understood I had simply entered God's kingdom as a disciple (a new follower) of Jesus!

Thus, based on clear scriptural teaching and collaborated by personal experience, I must categorically assert *there is no biblical salvation apart from being a disciple of Jesus*! If you have questions about this assertion, I hope explanations in following sections of the book will convince you of its validity.

Even though I stand firmly behind my assertion, I realize some readers may, in actuality, be functioning disciples without fully understanding their relationship with God as described by that term. God is much more interested in our heart's condition than our theological understanding. However, I believe a correct understanding of a person's biblical identity is a critical waypoint for a successful spiritual journey. Thus, my prayer and hope are that, as a result of reading this book, either you will fully understand and embrace your biblical identity as a disciple of Jesus, or, like I did, you will transition from your current journey to one in which you are a fully committed disciple of his.

Chapter 3
The Destination

In the previous chapter, I described the starting place for a spiritual journey that leads to God's planned destination. In this chapter, I will describe the destination.

As stated in the Introduction, when I use the phrase, "God's planned destination," I am not referring to "Heaven." Yes, the final physical destination for biblical Christians is Heaven. It will be a place of unimaginable splendor where God's majesty will be on full and continuous display. It will also be a place where we no longer suffer the limitations and ills of human life, and where we will spend eternity experiencing the fullness of love relationships our creator God desires for us. And based on who God is and his love for us, I can confidently speculate we will have meaningful and purposeful roles in the operation (and possible expansion) of God's eternal kingdom that will be far more significant than anything that can be experienced in this present life.

However, in this book, when I use "God's planned destination," I am referring to where God wants to take us on our spiritual journey during this life.

There are many scripture passages that provide insight into various aspects of God's plan for humanity. However, I believe God's planned destination for our spiritual journey can best be understood from the following scripture passage.

And we know that for those who love God all things work together for good, for those who are called according to his purpose. For those whom he foreknew he also predestined to be conformed to the image of his Son, in order that he might be the firstborn among many brothers.

Romans 8:28-29

We clearly learn from this passage that we are not an accident. We are not the mindless product of time and chance that some would have us believe. In God's foreknowledge, before he ever created anything, he knew us. I believe this includes our lineage, the time and place of our birth, our name – everything about us. Thus, we are here "according to his purpose."

We also learn that, as a loving Father, God desires that we come into his family, which includes "many brothers" (understood as both men and women).

When my wife and I got married, we both desired to have children. We wanted children to love and who returned our love. Motivated by love, we wanted what was best for them and tried to help them achieve that objective. However, because of human limitations, we didn't always know the best for them. Therefore, our efforts to help were sometimes counterproductive.

In a similar, but much superior way, God desires the best for his children, and he knows what is best! As we learn from Romans 8:28-29, *God's ultimate journey destination for those who belong to him is that they "be conformed to the image of his Son."*

Wow! This is almost beyond comprehension – *to be like Jesus*!

Again, as mentioned earlier, you may be thinking this only pertains to our final state in Heaven. However, notice the word "conformed" in the passage. To "be conformed" clearly implies a process. In multiple biblical passages, God is described as a potter and we as clay. We can't become like Jesus through our own ability, but God, as a potter, is able to conform us into the image he desires. Thus, we can understand that the process of being conformed to the image of Jesus starts when we become his follower and continues throughout our spiritual journey on planet Earth.

Can our conformity to the image of Jesus be fully realized in this life? Probably not, but through the enabling of the Holy Spirit, I firmly believe we can get much farther down that road than most followers of Jesus hope for or can even imagine.

Now we come full circle. In the previous chapter we concluded:

- All who experience biblical salvation are disciples (followers) of Jesus.
- All disciples have been set apart for God's purpose.
- As disciples mature, they take on the role of servants.

We can now understand that we start our spiritual journey to God's planned destination as disciples. As disciples we are set apart, "called according to his purpose." As we continue in our role as disciples of Jesus, our defining attributes become increasingly like his. As it was for him, our life focus is to serve (take on the role of a servant) our Father.

This includes living pure lives and being obedient to all he asks us to do. Our primary motivation for doing this is the same as Jesus' – love for our Father and for the people he created.

Each of you must now answer a question, "Are you currently traveling a spiritual journey that leads to God's planned destination?" If your answer is "yes," I hope you learn some things in the rest of the book that aid you in navigating the most direct route to God's planned destination.

If your answer is "no" or "I am not sure," the following parts of the book are designed to: 1) help you transition to God's planned journey, or 2) to give you confidence that you are already traveling it.

Part 2
Critical Waypoints for a Successful Journey

All professing Christians are on a spiritual journey to somewhere.

However, some may have started their journey based on faulty directions or incomplete understanding of those directions.

The Bible is the only trustworthy roadmap to navigate a successful spiritual journey.

This Part of the book describes critical biblical waypoints for a spiritual journey that leads to God's planned destination!

I realize these waypoints may be elementary to some readers, but even if this is the case, I suggest you review them to help solidify your biblical understanding.

Chapter 4
The Biblical Human Being

Using the Bible as the roadmap for our spiritual journey, the first waypoint we come to is our true identity as a created being. To ensure we arrive safely at God's planned destination, we must understand and fully embrace this identity!

OUR BEING

When we look at ourselves from a biblical perspective, what do we see? The first thing we see is human beings created in the "image of God." (Genesis 1:27).

The Bible describes God as an eternal spirit being with mind, will, and emotions (typically understood as "soul"). Therefore, as created in God's image, we can conclude that we are also spirit beings with souls. Since we had a beginning, we are not eternal in the sense that God is eternal, but we clearly see in scripture that our spirit being is immortal. (e.g., Matthew 25:31-46 and Revelation 20:11-15)

However, when we look in a mirror, we see a physical body. Based on scripture (Genesis 3) and experience, we know our physical body will die and cease to exist in its present form. We also know from scripture that our spirit being and physical body are separate entities, and our spirit being will leave our bodies at physical death. (2 Corinthians 5:6-9) Thus, we can conclude we are immortal spirit beings, with souls, who temporarily reside in physical bodies. We should not surmise, from this description, that we are destined to live eternally as disembodied spirit beings. The Bible tells us that at Jesus' second coming, all of God's people will be given new bodies, like Jesus' resurrected body (e.g., Romans 6:5, 1 Corinthians 15:49, and Philippians 3:20-21) .

In our human form, we are unique among all creatures of God's earthly creation. We alone have the ability to reason and relate to him. We were also created with the ability to choose how we live and relate to him. (In this respect, we are somewhat similar to angelic beings, who are also part of God's creation.)

However, our choices are strongly influenced by what the Bible describes as our "flesh." (Romans 7) The Greek word that translates to flesh can, depending on context, have different meanings. When it is used to describe human nature, we find "the flesh denotes mere human nature, the earthly nature of man apart from divine influence, and therefore prone to sin and opposed to God." [1]

Based on this definition, how can we understand our nature?

In my simple understanding, we have been designed by God with the ability to respond to certain physical and mental stimuli. We also have a strong propensity to gratify ourselves. However, because we can choose how we respond, our nature isn't intrinsically sinful. But, "apart from divine influence," our propensity to gratify ourselves will generally rule our choices and thereby result in sin.

In summary, we can therefore conclude that we are *immortal spirit beings, with souls, who temporarily reside in*

---

[1] (Smith 1999)

physical bodies, and who have a strong propensity to gratify
ourselves in ways that result in sin!

EXTERNAL & INTERNAL WITNESSES

We can understand other key attributes of our being by
consulting two scripture passages from the Bible.

Knowledge of God's Existence

For what can be known about God is plain to them,
because God has shown it to them. For his invisible
attributes, namely, his eternal power and divine
nature, have been clearly perceived, ever since the
creation of the world, in the things that have been
made. So they are without excuse.

Romans 1:19-20

This scripture passage describes knowledge that results
from observation of God's creation. Who has not somehow
sensed the existence of something or someone much bigger
and grander than themselves when viewing a particularly
awesome feature of God's creation? I will always remember
the times I saw the Grand Canyon and Niagara Falls. In these
situations, and in many others, I clearly perceived God's
majesty and power and even his presence.

This perception was also active in my life as a young boy.
I was raised on a ranch in central Texas where the intricacies
and beauty of nature were on constant display. Even at an
early age, it seemed obvious that what I was told about God
was true. It was natural and easy to believe!

In my role as an evangelist, I encountered only a few

hardcore, professing atheists. But when I questioned them about how they became atheists, they invariably pointed to circumstances and a time that led them to that position. This tells me that at one time they believed God existed but for some reason suppressed that knowledge, which is consistent with the above scripture.

Knowledge of Right and Wrong

For when Gentiles, who do not have the law, by nature do what the law requires, they are a law to themselves, even though they do not have the law. They show that the work of the law is written on their hearts, while their conscience also bears witness, and their conflicting thoughts accuse or even excuse them on that day when, according to my gospel, God judges the secrets of men by Christ Jesus.

Romans 2:14-16

This passage describes another intuitive attribute known as the human "conscience." Who can deny its existence? It regularly alerts us to wrong behavior and prompts us to do right. When we ignore it, we end up with guilty feelings and a sense of impending judgement.

It is obvious from observing very young children that this aspect or our being is something we were born with. However, it is also obvious that the naturally good function of our conscience can be corrupted by parental or societal influences. If we habitually ignore our conscience, it can become callous and hardened to the point where it no longer performs its designed function.

OUR PROBLEM

If we objectively examine our natural self, as illuminated by biblical light and life experiences, we see a problem we can't fix. Unless this problem is somehow resolved, we can't experience God's planned journey as previously described in Part 1 of this book.

The Root of Our Problem

As described above, we naturally have a strong propensity to gratify ourselves. When we choose to respond to stimuli in a way that gratifies ourselves but breaks God's law, the Bible says we sin! And we can be sure that our archenemies, Satan and his host of demons, are hell bent (no pun intended) to provide stimuli, uniquely designed for each individual, that entices us to sin.

We also know from experience that our conscience and our nature (our "flesh") perpetually conflict! Our conscience tells us what is right, but our flesh often gratifies itself in a way that violates our conscience.

The end result is that "all have sinned and fall short of the glory of God." (Romans 3:23) This is hard for us to accept because we all have a tendency to think that, although we may have some faults, we are basically good people. And if our good outweighs our bad, we will somehow be alright. However, the Bible paints a completely different picture. It says, "We have all become like one who is unclean, and all of our righteous deeds are like a polluted garment." (Isaiah 64:6)

If pressed, most people admit they have sinned. However, they may not fully internalize how serious sin is. In fact, some people laugh at sin. They think it is fun. Others think sin is like the flu - everyone gets it sooner or later, but eventually you get over it.

The Consequences of Our Problem

Although we don't like to admit it, our *sin always has consequences*! It is the root cause of all problems in the world. All the world's evils (wars, injustice, broken relationships, poverty, disease, etc.) can be traced to human sin. *Sin is serious*!

Sin is so serious that at one time, God destroyed all life on planet Earth except for one man, Noah, and his family. (Genesis 6-7) At another time, God completely destroyed two cities, Sodom and Gomorrah, along with all the people who lived there, because of their sinful lifestyles. (Genesis 19)

The Bible tells us that, under God's justice system, *"the wages of sin is death."* (Romans 6:23, emphasis added) Wages are what we earn and deserve. We are therefore faced with the reality that *the penalty we earn and deserve for our sin is death*! One day, we will suffer physical death because of God's judgement of Adam and Eve's sin. However, in the present, we can be physically alive but spiritually dead because of our sin. This means we are spiritually separated from God and therefore can't experience his love. The Bible describes our condition.

And you were dead in the trespasses and sins in which you once walked, following the course of this world, following the prince of the power of the air, the spirit that is now at work in the sons of disobedience—among whom we all once lived in the passions of our flesh, carrying out the desires of the body and the mind, and were by nature children of wrath, like the rest of mankind.

Ephesians 2:1-3

We see here that, because of our sin, we are *"children of wrath"* who must suffer God's righteous judgement. This judgement will occur at what is commonly called "The Great White Throne Judgement."

Then I saw a great white throne and him who was seated on it. From his presence earth and sky fled away, and no place was found for them. And I saw the dead, great and small, standing before the throne, and books were opened. Then another book was opened, which is the book of life. And the dead were judged by what was written in the books, according to what they had done. And the sea gave up the dead who were in it, Death and Hades gave up the dead who were in them, and they were judged, each one of them, according to what they had done. Then Death and Hades were thrown into the lake of fire. This is the second death, the lake of fire. And if anyone's name was not found written in the book of life, he was thrown into the lake of fire.

Revelation 20:11-15

Therefore, apart from divine influence, this is our natural predicament and there is not anything we can do to mitigate it!

But thankfully this isn't the end of the story. Because of God's grace and mercy, motivated by love, he did something for us we can't do ourselves. He made a way for us to be forgiven and thereby escape his judgement! We will learn how he did this in the next chapter.

Chapter 5
The Biblical God

The next critical waypoint for a successful spiritual journey is a biblical understanding of God. Most people in Judeo-Christian cultures have a general concept of God, but many times it is a product of their imagination or what they gleaned from uninformed sources. Thus, they may have created a "god" in their mind who doesn't really exist.

To understand who God really is, we must learn from the Bible. Apart from it, there are no credible sources of information about him. He is mentioned in some non-biblical historical and fictional writings, but none of them even touch the breadth of who he is. Only the Bible does this.

The biblical narrative begins with the statement, "In the beginning, God created the heavens and the earth." (Genesis 1:1) There are many so called "gods" in the world, but who is this particular God who created everything we know? This is a very broad subject. Volumes have and will be written about the biblical God, but in the interest of time and space, we will limit our discussion to what we must know to embark on a successful spiritual journey.

Many people throughout history have accused Christianity of being polytheistic (belief in multiple gods). However, the Bible is clear that there is only *one true God*! (Deuteronomy 4:35, 1 Kings 8:60, Isaiah 44:6, etc.)

Although the Bible states there is only one God, we clearly see him manifested in three persons throughout scripture. Thus, theologians coined the term "Trinity" to describe the biblical God. The first reference to the Triune God is probably in the first chapter of the Bible, where we read, "Then God said 'Let us make man in our image.'" (Genesis 1:26) Theologians generally agree that the "us" and "our" in this statement are probably referring to the three persons of God.

Although the Old Testament alludes to the Triune God, the identity of the three persons becomes much clearer in the New Testament.

> And when Jesus was baptized, immediately he went up from the water, and behold, the heavens were opened to him, and he saw the Spirit of God descending like a dove and coming to rest on him; and behold, a voice from heaven said, "This is my beloved Son, with whom I am well pleased."
>
> Matthew 3:16-17

> But he (Stephen), full of the Holy Spirit, gazed into heaven and saw the glory of God, and Jesus standing at the right hand of God.
>
> Acts 7:55 (parentheses added for clarity)

In both of these passages, we see God clearly depicted as three coexisting but distinct persons. Thus, we can understand there is one God, manifested in three persons – God the Father, God the Son, and God the Holy Spirit. This understanding is difficult for our finite human minds to fully comprehend but is an essential waypoint for a successful spiritual journey.

The following sections will attempt the impossible – to describe the three persons of the Trinity in a way that is fully comprehensible:

GOD THE FATHER

From the Bible, we can characterize God the Father as the overall orchestrator of the Trinity. In this role, he directs the Trinity's overall interactions with humanity. Jesus spoke clearly concerning this truth.

And he (God the Father) who sent me is with me. He has not left me alone, for I always do the things that are pleasing to him.

John 8:29 (parentheses added for clarity)

But the Helper, the Holy Spirit, whom the Father will send in my name, he will teach you all things and bring to your remembrance all that I have said to you.

John 14:26

No one can come to me unless the Father who sent me draws him. And I will raise him up on the last day.

John 6:44

These examples clearly portray God the Father's role as orchestrator, but in no way deny or imply lesser levels of deity for God the Son or God the Holy Spirit. The persons of the Trinity simply have different roles. I know this understanding of God is difficult to comprehend, but it's essential to a properly functioning relationship with him.

As overall orchestrator of the Trinity, God the Father has the following attributes in relationship to humanity:

- Self-Existent (without beginning or end, cause, or needs)
- Omniscient (all knowing)
- Omnipotent (all powerful)
- Omnipresent (always present everywhere)
- Immutable (unchangeable)
- Holy (absolute moral purity – manifested by perfect righteousness)
- Loving (unconditional concern for and promotion of our well-being)
- Just (absolutely right and fair in all actions related to us)
- Merciful (compassionate forbearance toward our imperfections)
- Gracious (desire and ability to bountifully give us that which we don't deserve)

When we contemplate these attributes, we stand in awe! Although some of us may have been fortunate to have relatively good earthly fathers, only God can provide the fatherhood each of us innately desires and needs. As such, he deeply desires to adopt us as his son or daughter. Later in the book, we will learn how this can happen.

GOD THE SON

Although we find many types and shadows of Jesus and prophecies about him throughout the Old Testament, he is only fully revealed in the New Testament. He is sometimes described in ways difficult to fully comprehend, but nevertheless true.

His Essence

From the New Testament we learn, "In the beginning was the Word, and the Word was with God, and the Word was God." (John 1:1) Furthermore, "the Word became flesh and dwelt among us." (John 1:14) Simply, this means *God came to earth in the human person of Jesus*. Therefore, in a way that is difficult to understand or explain, *he is both fully God and fully human*!

Unlike today, names in biblical times were often chosen to describe key attributes of a person. We can therefore learn more about Jesus by looking at the names and titles the Bible uses to describe him. Biblical scholars have identified some 200 names and titles used for Jesus in the Old and New Testaments. It is beyond the scope of this book to expound on all these references, but I will point to a few that directly pertain to the spiritual journey that is the subject of this book.

- Savior (Luke 2:11)
- Lamb of God (John 1:29)
- Good Shepherd (John 10:11, 14)
- Resurrection and the Life (John 11:25)
- The Way, and the Truth, and the Life (John 14:6)
- Deliverer (Romans 11:26)

- Mediator (1 Timothy 2:5)
- King of kings and Lord of lords (1 Timothy 6:15; Revelation 19:16)
- Great High Priest (Hebrews 4:14)
- Founder and Perfecter of our Faith (Hebrews 12:2)

The significance of these names and titles will become more meaningful as we continue.

His Human Life

He came to Earth as a fully human baby, supernaturally conceived in the womb of a young Jewish virgin woman named Mary. God, through an angel, instructed Joseph, who was engaged to Mary, to "call his name Jesus, for he will save his people from their sins." (Matthew 1:21) (The Greek name that translates to Jesus literally means "God is salvation.")

The angel also foretold Mary that Jesus would be "called the Son of the Most High." (Luke 1:32) This is consistent with the fact that he didn't have a human father.

There are a few biblical records of supernatural events surrounding his birth and early life (e.g., angels appearing to the shepherds, prophecies at his baptism, and a visit by wise men from the East), but nothing that gained widespread attention. As far as we know, he was raised as a normal Jewish boy, consistent with the culture and customs of his day.

However, at age 12, he amazed Jewish scholars with his knowledge of Old Testament scripture. (Luke 2:41-47) Although somewhat speculative, I believe his identity was progressively revealed to him as he studied prophecies about the coming Messiah. (Luke 2:52) Nevertheless, as truth was revealed to him, he had to receive and act on it by faith, as does any other human.

At age 30, his identity as the prophesied Messiah was confirmed by two events. When John the Baptist (the last of the Old Testament-type prophets) saw Jesus, he said, "Behold, the Lamb of God, who takes away the sin of the world!" (John 1:29) Then, when Jesus was baptized, God spoke from heaven and said, "This is my beloved Son, with whom I am well pleased." (Matthew 3:17)

Although he was called the "Son of God," he most often referred to himself as "Son of Man." (e.g., Matthew 12:8, Mark 14:21, Luke 19:10, John 3:13, etc.) Many scholars believe that when Jesus used the Son of Man designation, he was claiming to be the prophesied Messiah. (Daniel 7:13-14) Further, by using this designation, Jesus fully identified with our human condition. Being fully human, he was "tempted as we are, yet without sin." (Hebrews 4:15)

In his human form, he could "do nothing of his own accord, but only what he sees the Father doing." (John 5:19) In this respect, he was dependent on the Holy Spirit and had to live by faith just as any other human being must do.

Jesus fulfilled all the Messianic prophecies (over 200 by some counts) and further validated that he was God's Son by the miracles he performed. However, because he did not conform to the Messianic model the Jewish religious leaders incorrectly assumed, they refused to recognize Jesus for who he was and became increasingly jealous and hostile to his teaching. Eventually, they falsely accused him of blasphemy and convinced the Roman governor who had jurisdiction over them to order Jesus' crucifixion on a cross.

Following his crucifixion, Jesus' body was laid in a cave-type tomb that was typical for the elites of his day. A large stone was then rolled into place to close the entryway. The tomb was secured with a Roman seal and guarded by soldiers to prevent his disciples from stealing Jesus' body. Yet, on the third day following his death, an angel immobilized the guards and rolled back the stone to reveal an empty tomb. (Matthew 28:1-6) Jesus had been resurrected from the dead as prophesied! (Matthew 12:38-40)

His resurrection was validated by many eyewitnesses. (Matthew 28:1-10, 16-20 and 1 Corinthians 15:5-8.) During a period of forty days following his resurrection, he continued to validate his identity as the Messiah. He also continued to teach his followers about the kingdom of God and gave them instructions about what they were to do after he left this Earth. (Acts 1:3-8.)

Forty days after his resurrection, Jesus ascended to be with God his Father. (Acts 1:9-11, 7:55-56.) In a previous prophecy about this event, Jesus told his followers, "And if I go and prepare a place for you, I will come again and will take you to myself, that where I am you may be also." (John 14:3)

His Earthly Mission

God, in the person of Jesus, came to planet Earth for two specific purposes.

To Solve Humanity's Sin Problem

Shortly after beginning my spiritual journey at age 37, I found two other men in the small church I was attending, who were also new followers of Jesus. (I don't think this was a coincidence; I believe it was God-orchestrated.) As a result of our common newfound love for Jesus, we quickly formed a lifelong, close bond. We met regularly, shared what God was doing in our lives, jointly participated in various ministries, and generally encouraged and supported each other in our newfound faith.

One of the men had been a genuine (as opposed to a "drugstore" type) cowboy in his youth and young adulthood. He had been involved in a very rough and tumble lifestyle and profusely used the colorful language that typically went with it. After becoming a follower of Jesus, everything about him changed. As far as I know, he never said another curse word and became one of the most gentle, loving men I have ever known. He also began sharing his newfound faith with everyone he knew.

One day, he related a story about trying to share his faith with another ex-cowboy who had been one of his running buddies. While sitting with his buddy, he moved closer, got directly in his face, slapped him on the leg in typical cowboy fashion and said, "Cowboy, you need to get saved!"

The other cowboy's response was classic, "Saved from what?"

Every time I think about that scene, I can't help but chuckle! The story is silly but illustrates a critical question. What do we need to be saved from?

In the previous chapter, we described humanity's sin problem and its consequences. We learned that our sin earns God's wrath and prevents us from experiencing the love relationship he desires. The apostle John says it like this, "Whoever believes in the Son has eternal life; whoever does not obey the son shall not see life, but the wrath of God remains on him." (John 3:36) Thus, the answer to the cowboy's question is that we need to be *saved from God's wrath* that results from our disobedience (our sin)!

However, because of his love, he "is patient toward you, not wishing that any should perish, but that all should reach repentance." (2 Peter 3:9) Therefore, God did something for us we can't do for ourselves. He provided a solution for us to be saved from his wrath!

In the Old Testament, God instituted a sacrificial system to cover individual sins. This system seems crude to us today, but God wanted us to understand the seriousness of sin. Under that system, when a person sinned by breaking God's law, he or she had to bring an innocent, unblemished animal (e.g., a little lamb) to the temple. The person placed his or her hand on the lamb's head to symbolize transferring personal sin to the lamb, and then the priest slit the lamb's throat. The sacrifice of the innocent lamb paid the penalty for that individual's sin. Because people continued to sin, they had to do this over and over again. Although I obviously wasn't there, I can imagine the altar where the sacrifices were performed eventually became a big, bloody mess. I see this as a picture of today's world – a big bloody mess because of our sin!

Fortunately, the Old Testament sacrificial system was temporary. It was a picture (shadow) of God's ultimate solution to our sin problem.

Now, fast forward to the New Testament. John the Baptist was the last of the Old Testament-type prophets. His God-given role was to identify the prophesied Messiah (Savior).

When John the Baptist saw Jesus, he said, "Behold, the Lamb of God, who takes away the sin of the world!" (John 1:29)

Do you see the connection? When Jesus was crucified on the cross, he was the sacrifice for our sins. Because he was a perfect Lamb (without blemish), he paid the penalty for *all sins, for all people, for all time* (past, present, and future).

In doing this, the Bible explains, "He is the propitiation for our sins, and not for ours only but also for the sins of the whole world." (1 John 2:2) "Propitiation" is not a word we typically use in everyday conversation. But in the above scripture passage, it means God's wrath toward our sin has been appeased. In other words, Jesus suffered the wrath we legally deserve. In doing this, he made all the provisions that are necessary for our salvation!

We no longer have to be separated from God's love. We can be saved (rescued) from the penalty and power of sin. We can become spiritually alive ("born again," as described in John 3:3) and thereby reconciled to God. Thus, through his death on the cross, Jesus provides a way for us to experience all God planned, both in this life and in eternity!

To Initiate God's Kingdom

In addition to solving humanity's sin problem, Jesus fulfilled Old Testament prophecies about God's future kingdom, but not in the way Jewish people expected. He partially did this through miracles that demonstrated God's rule over his creation.

Further, he said, "The kingdom of God is not coming in ways that can be observed, nor will they say, 'Look, here it is!' or 'There!' for behold, the kingdom of God is in the midst of you." (Luke 17:20-21)

I recently attended the funeral for a close friend and brother in Christ. When it came my time to speak, I stated, "God's kingdom is where he rules, and Mel (my friend's name) lived in his kingdom." This was true because, based on the fruit of his life, it was obvious God ruled Mel's heart. Today, God rules spiritually in the hearts of all who belong to him. In this sense, Jesus ushered in an initial stage of God's kingdom.

His Current and Future Existence

Jesus, in his resurrected body, is currently seated at the right hand of God. (e.g. - Acts 7:56, Colossians 3:1, Romans 8:34, Hebrews 10:12, 1 Peter 3:22, and Revelation 5:7)

At Jesus's second coming, God's kingdom will be fully consummated. He will rule physically as "King of kings and Lord of lords," first on this present Earth for 1000 years, and eventually in "a new heaven and new earth" for all eternity. (Revelation 19:16, 20:1-6, and 21:1-4)

Although somewhat speculative, I see Jesus' existence in human form as particularly significant.

> Have this mind among yourselves, which is yours in Christ Jesus, who, though he was in the form of God, did not count equality with God a thing to be grasped, but emptied himself, by taking the form of a servant, being born in the likeness of men.
>
> Philippians 2:5-7

Most of the time, when expounders of God's Word

explain Jesus' sacrifice for us, they focus on the horrors of the cross. Sometimes, they add temporary separation from his Father as additional anguish he suffered on our behalf.

I, in no way, want to downplay or minimize the magnitude of these sacrifices. However, please think with me about his being "in the form of God," but voluntarily giving that position up to eternally exist "in the likeness of men." To me, that was at least as great a sacrifice as a onetime physical death or temporary separation from his Father.

GOD THE HOLY SPIRIT

The Holy Spirit is probably the most misunderstood person of the Triune God. For example, I sometimes hear the Holy Spirit referred to as "it" instead of "he." I cringe when I hear this because it is impossible to have a personal relationship with an "it."

Other times, I see him either neglected or overemphasized. Because of these extremes, some professing Christians are afraid to openly and honestly pursue a relationship with the Holy Spirit. They fear they will be viewed by others as either somehow lacking in their relationship with God, or even worse as some kind of fanatic. Thus, they proceed on what they perceive is the safest course, which is to avoid the subject.

However, a proper understanding of the Holy Spirit's role in a Jesus-follower's life is an essential waypoint for a successful spiritual journey. He is our guide and enabler for everything we can accomplish for God's kingdom. To gain this understanding, let's read what Jesus said about him.

When the Spirit of truth comes, he will guide you into all the truth, for he will not speak on his own authority, but whatever he hears he will speak, and he will declare to you the things that are to come. He will glorify me, for he will take what is mine and declare it to you.

John 16:13-14

Here, we see that the Holy Spirit is essential in helping us understand spiritual truth. In this respect, we can view him as a personal tutor and guide for our spiritual journey. Thus, to ensure a successful journey, we need to continually be open to his communication.

Sometimes, he communicates dramatically through dreams or visions, but he primarily speaks to us through hearing or reading God's Word, the Bible. When the Bible doesn't provide specific guidance for a given situation (e.g., where we are to live, what kind of profession or job we are to have, or who we are to marry), he speaks directly to our spirit – not in an audible voice, but in a way that can be clearly understood. I, along with all genuine followers of Jesus, can clearly testify about the Holy Spirit's specific guidance at critical times during our spiritual journeys. We can also testify about the Holy Spirit's conviction when we deviate from God's plan, either by engaging is some particular sin or departing from the course he has set before us.

To gain further understanding, let's read about how the apostle Paul describes the Holy Spirit's role in a Jesus follower's life.

But I say, walk by the Spirit, and you will not gratify the desires of the flesh. For the desires of the flesh are against the Spirit, and the desires of the Spirit are against the flesh, for these are opposed to each other, to keep you from doing the things you want to do.

Galatians 5:16-17

To each is given the manifestation of the Spirit for the common good. For to one is given through the Spirit the utterance of wisdom, and to another utterance of knowledge according to the same Spirit, to another faith by the same Spirit, to another gifts of healing by the same Spirit, to another working of miracles, to another prophecy, to another the ability to distinguish between spirits, to another various kinds of tongues, to another the interpretation of tongues. All these are empowered by the same Spirit, who apportions to each one individually as he wills.

1 Corinthians 12:7-11

Or do you not know that your body is the temple of the Holy Spirit within you, whom you have from God? You are not your own, for you have been bought with a price. So glorify God in your body.

1 Corinthians 6:19-20

In these scripture passages, we learn that the Holy Spirit's role in a Jesus follower's life is to help us overcome sin, to gift and empower us for ministry, and to help us conduct our lives in a way that glorifies God. *His role is essential to a successful spiritual journey!*

PERSONAL NOTE

Looking back on my spiritual journey during the past forty-plus years, I can see how my relationship with each person of the Triune God evolved to where it is today. I don't know if this evolution is typical, but I will share it as a point of reference.

I already shared about my life-changing encounter with God at age 37. Up until that encounter, I can't truly say I related specifically to any person of the Trinity. My beliefs were intellectual as opposed to relational. However, as a result of the encounter, that changed dramatically. Jesus became everything to me. He became my Lord (my owner, my master, my king, and my God). For about two years, the mere mention of his name brought tears of awe and joy. I reveled in his presence. Today, that relationship continues. It has mellowed somewhat in its emotional expression, but Jesus' Lordship is still the dominating factor that rules my life!

As a new follower of Jesus, I soon got involved in ministries of various types. As a result, I became exposed to the Holy Spirit in new and confounding ways. As a result, I was forced to examine my beliefs about him. As I studied the Bible, I realized I was missing a vital part of spiritual life. I needed to do something, but what?

Finally, in desperation, I went to the place in my home (my "altar") where I regularly met with God to discuss serious issues. My prayer that day was very simple, "God I want all that Peter and Paul had!"

That commenced an ongoing relationship with the Holy Spirit that continues to this day. Since then, I have learned to depend on his guidance and enabling to fulfill my role as an evangelist within the body of Christ. I also learned that when I "walk by the Spirit" (Galatians 5:16), I can trust my thoughts. I see this as the Holy Spirit's way of revealing truth and providing guidance during specific situations.

For example, sometimes when I ask God if I should do something (e.g., participate in a specific mission project), he answers with the question, "What do you want to do?"

I typically say, "I want to go," and the question is settled. (Of course, I always have to test my thoughts against the truth of scripture.)

I am now in the twilight of my life and, statistically, living in overtime. I find it somewhat ironic that, as I have aged physically, my need for a closer relationship with Father God has grown. I probably shouldn't be surprised by this. One day, I was talking to my 100-year-old mother. She previously suffered a stroke that led to all kinds of complications, both physical and mental.

One day, she asked me, "What can I do to get better?"

I struggled for an answer and finally replied, "Mother, you are 100 years old - at this point, I think all we can do is pray and leave your situation in God's hands."

She thought for a moment, looked me directly in the eyes, and spontaneously said one of the most beautiful prayers I ever heard, "Father, please come to get me!"

Today, when I am facing life issues that have no obvious solution, similar prayers come to my mind. Sometimes, I can almost see myself as a small boy running to my Father who sweeps me into his arms and says, "It will be alright—I have the situation under control."

Chapter 6
The Biblical Gospel

In contemporary Christian evangelism, the gospel is generally presented as the "good news" that God came to planet Earth in the person of Jesus to pay the penalty for human sin. As a result, if we "accept Jesus as our Savior," we will be "saved." As such, our sins are forgiven, and we can spend eternity in Heaven with God. This is the gospel message I heard all my life and, up until a few years ago, passed on to thousands of people in many parts of the world.

As we learned in the previous chapter, it is certainly true that God came to Earth in the person of Jesus to pay the penalty for human sin. And it's certainly true that Jesus can be our Savior. But, as I have contemplated the gospel more thoroughly during the past several years, I believe contemporary evangelism approaches have largely understated the full scope of the gospel message. I believe the gospel is *much better news* than many have understood and proclaimed!

The apostle Paul said the gospel is the *"power of God for salvation* to everyone who believes." (Romans 1:16, emphasis added) What is this "power of God for salvation?" I believe it can generally be categorized as the following.

POWER TO TRANSFORM

Whether we realize it or not, each of us desperately needs transformation. As we discover through life experiences, we are incapable of transforming ourselves. We need to be transformed from an "old self" to a "new self." (Ephesians 4:17-24) The old self is our natural state apart from God's intervention. In this state, we are "slaves of sin," resulting in spiritual "death." (Romans 6:20-21) This means we are separated from the God who created and loves us. Consequently, we can't satisfy our deepest, innate desire for a full and meaningful life that can only come from a personal relationship with our Creator.

In stark contrast, the "new self" is God's perfect design for his creation. Through God's transforming power, we are "born again," or equivalently, "born of God." (John 3:1-8 and 1 John 5:4, 18) As such, we are "a new creation" in which the "old has passed away" and "the new has come." (2 Corinthians 5:17) As God's new creation, we have a completely new identity. We have been transformed from sinners into saints. Now God is our Father and we are eternally part of his family. We have been delivered from the kingdom of Satan and brought into the kingdom of God. In this state, we can experience the full and meaningful life God created for us to have.

POWER TO OVERCOME

Although we are new creations with a new spiritual identity, obstacles must be overcome to fully experience this identity. These obstacles can be physical or spiritual. They can generally be categorized in one of the following ways.

Natural Propensity to Sin

The natural tendencies of our "flesh" is a major obstacle that must be overcome in order to live as God intends. (Romans 8) As described earlier in this book, our flesh is designed to respond to certain physical and mental stimuli and has a strong propensity to gratify itself. In our natural state, apart from divine influence, our propensity to gratify ourselves will rule our life choices in ways that break God's laws and result in sin.

However, as newborn sons or daughters of God and followers of Jesus, we are no longer in our natural state – we are new creations. As such, our body has become "a temple of the Holy Spirit." (1 Corinthians 6:19) When we "walk by the Spirit," we "will not gratify the desires of the flesh." (Galatians 5:16) Therefore, to the degree that we walk by the Spirit, we can overcome sin! We may not do this perfectly, but as God's "workmanship," we can and should be continually moving toward that goal. (Ephesians 2:10)

Trials of Life

None of us can escape trials that result from living in a fallen world. These trials come in all shapes and sizes. They can be the result of such things as birth abnormalities, physical accidents, prejudices, injustices, persecutions, relationship, financial and health issues. Yet, we are instructed to "Count it all joy... when you meet trials of various kinds." (James 1:2) In our natural ability, we are incapable of doing this. However, through the power of the indwelling Holy Spirit, we can do as God instructs, realizing that "the testing of your faith produces steadfastness... that you may be perfect and complete, lacking in nothing." (James 1:3-4)

Who has not been amazed when observing someone with serious physical or mental issues who is obviously living above their circumstances? Although human willpower can sometimes achieve this to a degree, only God's gracious power is sufficient to "be perfect and complete, lacking in nothing."

Spiritual Battles

Ever since Adam and Eve's abdication of their God-ordained responsibility in the Garden of Eden, planet Earth has been ruled by Satan and his host of demons. As enemies of God, they are also enemies of all who belong to him. Their goal is to cause enmity between us and God, or at the very least, to hinder our effectiveness in fulfilling God's plan for our lives. They have some God-limited ability to directly impact our physical circumstances and thought processes. They use this ability to inject temptations, doubts, and fear into our lives. However, as we walk by the Spirit, we have God's power to "resist the devil" and thereby effectively counter his attacks. (James 4:7)

One of Satan's primary strategies is to establish sin strongholds in our lives. These strongholds can take many forms. They include such things as false beliefs, substance abuse, sexual obsessions or perversions, unhealthy relationships, and uncontrolled anger. Once these strongholds have been firmly established, human willpower is insufficient to break them. However, since we have the indwelling Holy Spirit, all genuine followers of Jesus can say with the apostle Paul, "For though we walk in the flesh…the weapons of our warfare are not of the flesh but have divine power to destroy strongholds." (2 Corinthians 10:3-4) Along with multitudes of Jesus-followers throughout Christian history, I can attest to the Holy Spirit's power to destroy sin strongholds.

Another of our enemy's primary strategies is to use societal influences and pressures to distract us from following biblical guidelines for living in God's creation. During my time on planet Earth, I have witnessed an exponential erosion of biblical morality. Our entertainment industry is a major factor in this erosion. It seems that every year, much of our available entertainment becomes increasingly hostile to biblical values. Miraculously, the Holy Spirit's power, working in and through us, is sufficient to overcome these influences.

POWER TO ENABLE

One of the saddest things I see within the body of Christ is longtime professing Christians who have never found the reason God put them on planet Earth. As a result, their lives are basically being wasted. This is not the way God designed for his chosen people to live.

The Bible teaches that each follower of Jesus is uniquely gifted by the Holy Spirit to perform one or more functions within the body of Christ. (1 Corinthians 12) We are also described as "ambassadors for Christ." (2 Corinthians 5:20) We have both important functions to perform within the body of Christ and a mandate to represent the kingdom of God to the outside world! In our own ability, we are incapable of fulfilling these roles. But through the Holy Spirit's enabling, we can be and do all God desires.

PERSONAL NOTE

The above gospel description is not an abstract theoretical construct; it is practical for everyday life! I, along with all genuine Jesus-followers, can readily testify about God's transforming, overcoming, and enabling power on a consistent basis. If you are not currently experiencing this power in your life, I strongly suggest you assess the validity of your relationship with God!

Chapter 7
Biblical Salvation

In the previous chapter, we learned that biblical salvation is much more than just a ticket to heaven. So how do we experience the fullness of biblical salvation? Thankfully, the Bible provides a clear answer to this question.

> But God, being rich in mercy, because of the great love with which he loved us, even when we were dead in our trespasses, made us alive together with Christ—by grace you have been saved—and raised us up with him and seated us with him in the heavenly places in Christ Jesus, so that in the coming ages he might show the immeasurable riches of his grace in kindness toward us in Christ Jesus. For by grace you have been saved through faith. And this is not your own doing; it is the gift of God, not a result of works, so that no one may boast. For we are his workmanship, created in Christ Jesus for good works, which God prepared beforehand, that we should walk in them.
>
> Ephesians 2:4-10

From this scripture passage, we can conclude that those who have experienced biblical salvation have been:

- Saved because of God's mercy and love.
- Saved by God's grace.
- Saved through faith.
- Saved for good works.

Let's expound these conclusions to better understand biblical salvation.

GOD'S MERCY AND LOVE

The first things we see in the above Ephesians passage is God's "mercy" and "the great love with which he loved us." It's clear throughout scripture that we are the beneficiaries of God's mercy and love. We see this in the Garden of Eden where he obviously desired and fostered a personal relationship with Adam and Eve. We see it when he chose Abraham to be the progenitor of his chosen people. We see it in how he dealt with his chosen people throughout Old Testament history. However, we see it more clearly here, in the New Testament, where God loves us even when we are "dead in our trespasses." We can't do anything to either increase or diminish his love. *He loves us because of who he is!*

To experience God's love, we must receive it. We must let him love us! When we do this, we naturally love him in return. Please let me illustrate.

At the age of 13, while in the eighth grade of school, I fell in love with a girl who eventually became my wife. Even at that early age, I remember thinking she was the person I wanted to spend my life with. As a result of my love, I pursued her. However, it soon became obvious she was not as interested in me as I was in her. I had a few dates with her in high school, but it was obvious my feelings for her were not reciprocated. I'm not sure of the reason. Maybe she questioned my intentions or whether I had her best interests at heart. As a result, maybe she was afraid to fully trust me. For whatever reason, she would not receive my love. She would not let me love her!

After high school, I continued to pursue the love of my life. Finally, through a set of circumstances I won't take time to describe, her attitude toward me changed. She became open to receiving my love. As a result, she loved me in return! Finally, at age 19 (it took six long years to "catch" her), we arrived at a mutual agreement to stand before a minister where I said "I do," she said "I do," and we entered into a lifelong, love-relationship as husband and wife.

As part of the marriage ceremony, the minister quoted from the Bible, "Therefore a man shall leave his father and his mother and hold fast to his wife, and they shall become one flesh." (Genesis 2:24) We clearly understood that this meant we were to put each other as first among all human relationships. As part of this commitment, it was also clearly understood that any other lovers in either of our lives wouldn't be acceptable. Because of our love for each other, we were very willing to make this commitment.

As I write this book, my wife and I have been married for over sixty years. Over the years, as we fulfilled our commitments, our relationship has grown richer and deeper. At this point, I can't imagine life without her. Even though we sometimes see life situations differently, there is a settled oneness in our relationship that is unshakable. I fully trust her even as she trusts me.

So why did I share this story? I have come to understand that God designed his creation in such a way as to reveal himself. This is why Jesus consistently used parables about everyday life to illustrate spiritual truths. In the same way, I see marriage as a picture of what a love relationship with God is like.

If you think back over your life, you will realize God has continually pursued you – maybe through other people, things you have seen and read, unique life experiences, etc. He has been trying to make his love known to you. Maybe you understand this intellectually, but haven't yet come to the place where you fully trust him. As a result, you haven't received his love and therefore haven't begun to love him in return!

However, that can change! Hopefully, as a result of reading this book, you have begun to see God and his commitment to your well-being more clearly. As a result, you may choose to trust him and let him love you. When you do this, you will naturally love him in return.

As in the marriage illustration, when you commence a personal relationship with God, you must be willing to place God first in your life. Anything less in unacceptable to him. He will not be content for there to be any other lovers (anything that takes priority over your relationship with him) in your life!

In contemplating this, all we can do is bow in awe. As insignificant and undeserving as we may seem, the Creator of everything we know loves us and desires that we love him.

GOD'S GRACE

As an evangelist, I have interacted with people from many different cultures throughout the world. In this role, I have observed a common belief system among those who believe in some kind of deity. The general concept is that their deity has a set of scales. All the "good" things they do go on one side of the scale, and the "bad" things go on the other side. If the good outweighs the bad, they earn favor with their deity. It's sad but true that this same general concept has been adopted by many professing Christians but is in direct opposition to biblical assertions. From the Ephesians passage, we can clearly understand that we can't be saved by anything we merit, but only by God's grace.

Grace can be understood as God's unmerited favor, or equivalently, God doing for us that which we can't do and don't deserve. For example, we may train all our lives and become the best human swimmer who ever existed. But we will never be able to swim nonstop across the Atlantic Ocean. It's humanly impossible. Similarly, no matter how hard we try or how good we could be, we can never merit salvation. Only God can save us, and he offers to do it as a gift. He can justly do this because, as explained in Chapter 5, Jesus paid the purchase price for our salvation. He did this as an act of love by dying on the cross to satisfy God's penalty for our sin.

As we learned in the previous chapter, God's saving grace not only provides a ticket to Heaven, it also includes power for us to live as he desires during our time on planet Earth. Since God has done everything required for our salvation, what do we need to do?

OUR FAITH

Although we are saved because of God's love and by his grace, it is also clear from the Ephesians passage that we have a role in our salvation. We are "saved through faith." This means, to experience salvation, we must receive God's gift of salvation by faith. This understanding is consistent throughout the New Testament, where we see that "justification by faith" is the only standard by which we can have a right standing with God. (e.g., see Romans 3:21-26, Galatians 3:8-9, and Philippians 3:8-9)

The doctrine of justification by faith is unique to biblical Christianity. All other religions require adherence to some set of rituals or rules to obtain favor with their deity. However, as a functioning evangelist within the body of Christ for the past forty-plus years, I observe salvation faith as being often misrepresented in contemporary gospel messages. This is partly due to limitations of the English language that sometimes doesn't clearly distinguish between "belief" and "faith" but also is the result of overzealous attempts to gain new converts.

Jesus often used parables to teach spiritual truths. I will use a similar approach in an attempt to clarify biblical faith that is essential for salvation and progress during the ensuing spiritual journey.

I found the following supposedly true story on the internet.

> Can you imagine a tightrope stretched over a quarter of a mile and spanning the breadth of Niagara Falls? The thundering sound of the

pounding water drowning out all other sounds as you watch a man step onto the rope and walk across!

This stunning feat made Charles Blondin famous in the summer of 1859. He walked 160 feet above the falls several times back and forth between Canada and the United States as huge crowds on both sides looked on with shock and awe. Once he crossed in a sack, once on stilts, another time on a bicycle, and once he even carried a stove and cooked an omelet!

On July 15, Blondin walked backward across the tightrope to Canada and returned pushing a wheelbarrow.

The Blondin story is told that it was after pushing a wheelbarrow across while blindfolded that Blondin asked for some audience participation. The crowds had watched and 'Ooooohed' and 'Aaaaahed!' He had proven that he could do it; of that, there was no doubt. But now he was asking for a volunteer to get into the wheelbarrow and take a ride across the Falls with him!

It is said that he asked his audience, 'Do you believe I can carry a person across in this wheelbarrow?' Of course, the crowd shouted that yes, they believed!

It was then that Blondin posed the question – 'Who will get in the wheelbarrow?'

Of course, none did. [2]

This story illustrates the difference between head belief and heart belief. Notice that the crowd said they believed, but none were willing to get into the wheelbarrow. Because they were unwilling to get into the wheelbarrow, they demonstrated that they only had head belief, perhaps better understood as intellectual belief. To be truthful, I wouldn't have gotten into the wheelbarrow either, because there is no human being that I am willing to put that much trust in. However, if Jesus clearly asked me to get into his "wheelbarrow" today, I would do it because I trust his ability to safely take me wherever he desires.

For the twenty-five years between ages 12 and 37, I didn't have this kind of trust in Jesus. I intellectually believed some biblical facts about him, but my beliefs did not materially affect the way I lived. But at age 37, my beliefs moved from my head to my heart. This changed everything! My beliefs became the foundation for how I lived. I had finally gotten into Jesus' "wheelbarrow" and let him take me wherever he desired!

With this background, let's go to the Romans 10:5-13 passage that describes heart belief. The essence of this passage can be summarized.

> "The word is near you, in your mouth and in your heart" (that is, the word of faith that we proclaim); because, if you confess with your mouth that Jesus is Lord and believe in your heart that God raised him from the dead, you

---

[2] (Creative Bible Study n.d.)

will be saved. For with the heart one believes and is justified, and with the mouth one confesses and is saved.

Romans 10:8-10

Since we are "justified by faith," we can understand from this passage that heart belief and faith are equivalent. Thus, in respect to biblical salvation, genuine heart belief (faith) naturally leads to a confession that "*Jesus is Lord*!"

Depending on context, the transliterated Greek word that translates to "Lord" can mean *owner, master, sovereign (king), or God*.[3] In the context of biblical salvation, it includes all of these meanings! Therefore, to experience genuine salvation, Jesus must *be Lord*! We must be willing to get into the unique "wheelbarrow" he planned for our life and be willing to let him take us wherever he desires.

If Jesus is truly our Lord (our owner, master, king, and God), we have no choice but to do this. We must follow him (be his disciple) wherever he leads!

OUR GOOD WORKS

Some years ago, I led a men's study group at the church I attended. It was a study that involved a lot of round-table type discussion. During the discussion, it became obvious that some (probably most) of the men's primary focus was on a person's salvation experience. How a person conducted their life afterward was of lesser importance. I had previously heard similar sentiments routinely expressed, but

---

[3] (Smith, Greek Lexicon entry for Kurios 1999)

for some reason, this particular discussion instantly initiated flashing red lights in my spirit. As an evangelist, with my emphasis on a salvation decision, had I unconsciously been promoting this type of belief system?

To address this issue, let's return to the Ephesians passage where we read, "For we are his workmanship, created in Christ Jesus for good works, which God prepared beforehand that we should walk in them." When we examine this verse in its context, we see a clear relationship between salvation faith and the "good works" God planned for us to do in life.

In order to better understand this relationship, let's look at the following scripture passage.

> What good is it, my brothers, if someone says he has faith but does not have works? Can that faith save him? If a brother or sister is poorly clothed and lacking in daily food, and one of you says to them, "Go in peace, be warmed and filled," without giving them the things needed for the body, what good is that? So also faith by itself, if it does not have works, is dead.
>
> James 2:14-17

This passage is talking about "works" associated with salvation faith. At first glance the James passage may seem to contradict the "gift" aspect of salvation in the Ephesians passage. But notice the little word "says" in the first sentence of the James passage. With the addition of this word, James differentiates between someone "saying" they have faith and someone actually having faith. With this understanding, we can conclude that James is explaining that genuine salvation faith will always be evident in the way a person lives. Their "works" will demonstrate that their salvation is genuine. In other words, *salvation and how we conduct our lives afterward are inseparable!*

This interpretation of the James passage is well supported by many other scripture passages throughout the New Testament. A few applicable passages include these.

> Either make the tree good and its fruit good, or make the tree bad and its fruit bad, for the tree is known by its fruit.
>
> Matthew 12:33

> As obedient children, do not be conformed to the passions of your former ignorance, but as he who called you is holy, you also be holy in all your conduct, since it is written, "You shall be holy, for I am holy."
>
> 1 Peter 1:14-16

> And by this we know that we have come to know him, if we keep his commandments.
>
> 1 John 2:3

Based on these and many other passages that could be cited, we can confidently conclude that genuine salvation always results in some type of "good works." These works are therefore evidence that genuine salvation occurred.

The bottom line is that we are saved through faith alone, but faith without works is an oxymoron. *As James said, "faith by itself, if it does not have works, is dead!"*

OTHER ASPECTS OF SALVATION

In addition to the Ephesians passage, we find scripture passages that explain other aspects of biblical salvation that must be considered in becoming a follower (disciple) of Jesus.

The Costs of Salvation

As discussed above, the Bible clearly describes biblical salvation as a free gift from our creator God. Even though salvation is a gift, it can be the costliest present we ever receive!

Jesus addressed this cost for those who considered following him.

> Whoever does not bear his own cross and come after me cannot be my disciple. For which of you, desiring to build a tower, does not first sit down and count the cost, whether he has enough to complete it? Otherwise, when he has laid a foundation and is not able to finish, all who see it begin to mock him, saying, 'This man began to build and was not able to finish.'
>
> Luke 14:27-30

Thus, in scripture, we see that biblical salvation has both "gift" and "cost" aspects.

Based on experience as an evangelist, I believe an over-focus on the gift aspect of salvation can lead to an "easy believe" type of salvation, which is seductively appealing but dangerously misleading. We need to understand that salvation is a free gift but *only in the sense that it can't be earned or deserved*!

To illustrate this understanding, let's look at Jesus' last command to his followers (commonly referred to as the Great Commission), "Go therefore and make disciples of all nations." (Matthew 28:19) As described in Part 1, the execution of this command started in the book of Acts where *all* who experienced biblical salvation were described as disciples. These new followers of Jesus were obviously immature, but their lives had been fundamentally transformed by the free gift of eternal life they received. As they matured into servants of God, he used them to accomplish his kingdom objectives. As we read about them in the Bible, it is obvious they suffered substantial personal costs. Many even suffered the ultimate cost of being martyred for their faith.

God's plan has not changed! Today, when we receive the gift of eternal life, we become transformed followers (disciples) of Jesus. As we mature, we too assume the role of servants whom God uses to accomplish his purpose in today's world.

Although the benefits of eternal life far out-weighs anything negative we might experience on this Earth, we too can expect to suffer substantial, consequential costs associated with our role as servants of God. Today, these costs can typically be measured in terms of lifestyle changes, personal relationships, time commitments, financial priorities, persecution, etc. All genuine Jesus-followers can readily testify to the ongoing reality of these types of costs.

But we can also testify that current benefits and promised future rewards far outweigh any costs we have incurred.

In the U.S., persecution costs are generally limited to various forms of rejection, ridicule, intolerance, and discrimination. However, in some other parts of the world, martyrdom is increasingly common. Based on current trends, who knows what the future holds?

With that in mind, making a decision to become a disciple of Jesus, and thereby experience biblical salvation, we must carefully "count the cost."

The Role of Repentance in Salvation

We previously discussed the universality of humanity's sin problem that results in spiritual death. Once we fully embrace the fact that we are spiritually dead and desperately need to be rescued, we will naturally experience a special kind of grief that leads to biblical repentance.

Most people do not have a complete understanding of what repentance means. People generally associate it with guilt feelings for the wrongs they have done. Although repentance certainly includes guilt feelings, it encompasses much more. Using basic study tools, we find that the original Greek word that translates to "repentance" can be understood as "a change of mind." [4]

With this understanding, let's look at an example of how the Bible uses it.

> For godly grief produces a repentance that leads
> to salvation without regret, whereas worldly

[4] (Smith, Greek Lexicon entry for Melanoia 1999)

grief produces death.

2 Corinthians 7:10

Thus, repentance can be understood as a changing of our mind that leads to salvation. For years, because of my disobedience and sinful lifestyle, I experienced a "worldly grief." (Some Bible translations use "sorrow" instead of "grief," which is more descriptive for me.) However, the worldly sorrow I experienced only resulted in an increasingly heavy load of guilt. This guilt caused both emotional and physical distress to the point that I could not continue in the way I was going. Something had to change! I now realize God let me reap what I had sown to get my attention. This godly sorrow I was experiencing eventually led me to see my sin as God saw it. And I didn't like what I saw!

I saw how my sin was affecting my relationship with God and with other people. As a result, I changed my mind about how I wanted to live the rest of my life.

Finally, at age 37, my repentance was completed when I asked God to forgive me and told him, regardless of where it took me or the costs of going there, I wanted to be a follower of Jesus for the rest of my life. Because of my heart attitude, as expressed by that simple prayer, I was supernaturally and instantly transformed from believer in Jesus to follower (disciple) of Jesus.

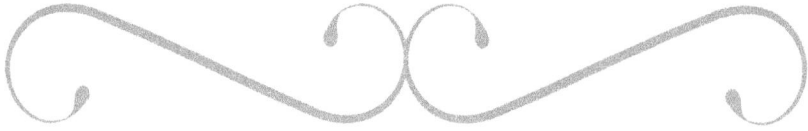

Part 3
The Journey

Now that we have adopted the Bible as our roadmap and have examined critical waypoints necessary for a successful spiritual journey, we are ready to proceed.

This Part of the book will explain how we can begin and navigate a spiritual journey that leads to God's planned destination on planet Earth and eventually, to spend eternity with him in Heaven!

Chapter 8
Beginning the Journey

In preparation for beginning a spiritual journey that leads to God's planned destination, let's review what we learned to this point.

In Part 1, we learned:

- We are the pinnacle of God's creation plan, but can only experience his plan by traveling the spiritual journey he uniquely designed for each of us.
- Our spiritual journey begins as a disciple (follower) of Jesus and proceeds toward the destination of being "conformed to the image of his Son (Jesus)."
- As we become increasingly more like Jesus, we take on the role of servants, who God can use to accomplish his kingdom objectives on planet Earth.

In Part 2, we learned that God made all the provisions required for us to embark on a spiritual journey that leads to his planned destination, and invites to do so. But we must count the costs of being a genuine Jesus-follower and choose our response.

SELF-EXAMINATION

The question now becomes, "Where do I *really* stand in my relationship with God?" To answer this question, the Bible tells us.

> Examine yourselves to see whether you are in the faith. Test yourselves. Or do you not realize this about yourselves, that Jesus Christ is in you?—unless indeed you fail to meet the test!
>
> 2 Corinthians 13:5

I fully realize that some (maybe most) readers are already functioning disciples of Jesus. Some may have even matured to the point where, like some of the biblical authors, you can describe yourselves as servants of God/Jesus. (Romans 1:1; James 1:1; 2 Peter 1:1; Jude 1:1) If so, I rejoice that you are my brother or sister in Christ, wish you well on the remainder of your journey, and look forward to spending eternity with you.

However, based on personal experience and observations, it is likely that some readers are professing Christians who can't honestly describe themselves as genuine followers (disciples) of Jesus. This was my case from ages 12 to 37. At age 12, I walked down the aisle of a small rural church in response to a gospel message and invitation. The invitation wasn't very clear as to the commitment I was making, but I somehow felt a need to respond. A few weeks later, I was baptized in a local creek and became an official "Christian" and church member.

Looking back, I can't honestly say that anything in my life really changed. Jesus said, "the tree is known by its fruit." (Matthew 12:33) The fruit of my life during that time span can, at best, be described as stunted or diseased. Based on that evidence, I have serious questions about my spiritual status during those years of my life. Maybe you can identify with my experience and realize you need to return to ground zero and begin anew a spiritual journey that ensures your arrival at God's planned destination.

REQUIREMENTS TO BE A DISCIPLE

So, what are Jesus' requirements for being his disciple? We can gain insight by looking at some of his statements to those who were considering following him.

If anyone would come after me, let him deny himself and take up his cross and follow me.

Matthew 16:24

A disciple is not above his teacher, but everyone when he is fully trained will be like his teacher.

Luke 6:40

If you abide in my word, you are truly my disciples, and you will know the truth, and the truth will set you free.

John 8:31-32

By this all people will know that you are my disciples, if you have love for one another.

John 13:35

By this my Father is glorified, that you bear much fruit and so prove to be my disciples.

John 15:8

As we look at these requirements, it can be almost

overwhelming to think about trying to meet them. Is it even possible?

In consideration of this all-important commitment, we need to understand and fully embrace the fact that, "With man this is impossible, but with God all things are possible." (Matthew 19:26) To accomplish the impossible, we must be absolutely dependent on the Holy Spirit to guide and enable us in fulfilling Jesus' requirements.

It also helps to remember that the definition of a disciple does not carry connotations of maturity. As previously explained, disciples are simply pupils who made a commitment to follow and learn from their teacher! As new disciples, we are like the original disciples. We stumble and sometimes fall. But as we persevere with the Holy Spirit's help, we mature and become increasingly more like our teacher.

INVITATION TO BE A DISCIPLE

So where do you find yourself today? Can you honestly describe yourself as a disciple of Jesus? If your answer is "no" or "I'm not sure," do you sense Jesus inviting (calling) you to become his disciple? If so, please carefully consider the following, previously referenced scripture passage.

"The word is near you, in your mouth and in your heart" (that is the word of faith that we proclaim); because if you confess with your mouth that Jesus is Lord and believe in your heart that God raised him from the dead, you will be saved. For with the heart one believes and is justified, and with the mouth one confesses and is saved.

Romans 10:8-10

Based on this scripture, we see a combination of two things that clearly result in biblical salvation:

- Believe in our heart that God raised Jesus from the dead.
- Confess with our mouth that Jesus is Lord.

As explained earlier in the book, heart belief is equivalent to biblical faith. It includes intellectual belief but goes much further. In regard to biblical salvation, it produces a profound transformation in the way you perceive and relate to God and his creation plan for humanity. It forever changes the way you conduct your life from that point forward!

Also, please understand that just saying "Jesus is Lord" is not necessarily a confession that Jesus is Lord. Jesus made this clear by saying, "Not everyone who says to me 'Lord, Lord,' will enter the kingdom of heaven, but the one who does the will of my Father who is in heaven." (Matthew 7:21) To experience genuine salvation, Jesus must *be Lord*! As previously explained in Chapter 7, the Greek word that translates to "Lord" can mean *owner, master, sovereign (king),* or *God,* depending on the context. However, in the context of biblical salvation, it includes all of these meanings!

With these qualifiers, my questions to you are:

- Do you believe in your heart (not just in your head) that Jesus is alive? (If he is alive, he is someone you can know and follow!)
- Are you willing to confess with your mouth that you want Jesus to be your Lord (your owner, master, king, and God)?

If your answer to these questions is an unqualified "yes," please carefully consider the following example prayer.

> *Lord God, I have messed up my life. I've believed intellectually, but haven't lived as a follower of Jesus. Please forgive me! At this moment, I want to set things right. I want to transition from the journey I have been traveling to the one you planned for me. Whatever it means and wherever it takes me, I choose, starting now and for the rest of my life, to follow Jesus as my Savior and Lord. In his name I pray – Amen!*

Does this prayer honestly express the desire of your heart? If so, you can do like I did when I was 37 years old. You can pray this or a similar prayer as *your confession that Jesus is Lord*!

If your prayer is from your heart, God's Word says, "**You will be saved**!" As such, you belong to God. He becomes your Father and you become his son or daughter. You are "born again to a living hope." (1 Peter 1:3) You become "a new creation." (2 Corinthians 5:17) And you become one of Jesus' "disciples" (follower). (Matthew 28:19-20)

Did you honestly pray the prayer as your confession that Jesus is your Lord? If so, welcome to God's family and kingdom! Now that you have experienced biblical salvation, you can assume your identity as a disciple of Jesus and begin living like the new creation you have become! Run your race well, and you, along with all other genuine followers of Jesus, will receive the reward God has planned for you.

> Blessed be the God and Father of our Lord Jesus Christ! According to his great mercy, he has caused us to be born again to a living hope through the resurrection of Jesus Christ from the dead, to an inheritance that is imperishable, undefiled, and unfading, kept in heaven for you, who by God's power are being guarded through faith for a salvation ready to be revealed in the last time.
>
> 1 Peter 1:3-5

Chapter 9
First Steps

This chapter was written for: 1) those who have become new followers of Jesus as a result of reading this book, and 2) those who were already followers of Jesus before reading the book, but currently find themselves somehow struggling on their spiritual journey and wondering what they should do.

If you are in the first category, please understand your first steps are extremely critical to a successful spiritual journey.

If you are in category two, I suggest you may need to return to "ground zero" and take some critical first steps you may have missed.

I realize some of the steps described in following sections are subject to diverse interpretation and application among various church traditions. However, multitudes of others and I have found the steps, as generally described, to be crucial for successful journeys. Therefore, I suggest you approach the chapter with an open mind and Bible to let God convince you of how you should proceed.

BE BAPTIZED

Among the various Christian traditions, there is much confusion about biblical baptism. As an example, I have often heard my wife testify about her baptism experiences.

As a youth, she was "sprinkled" as part of a church confirmation process. After we married, she adopted my church tradition that required "immersion" to join. Later, she realized she had not truly experienced biblical salvation and was baptized again as a new disciple (follower) of Jesus. These kinds of confusion about the practice of baptism are not unusual.

To help clarify such confusion, let's first review the Matthew 28:18-20 passage (commonly referred to as "The Great Commission") where we find Jesus' final mandates to his original disciples.

- Make disciples of all nations.
- Baptize them in the name of the Father, Son, and Holy Spirit.
- Teach them to observe all that I have commanded you.

Note the order of Jesus' mandates.

1. They were first to become disciples (experience biblical salvation as described in the previous chapter).
2. After they became disciples, they were then to be baptized.
3. As baptized disciples, they were then to be taught to observe all of Jesus' commandments (how to live as followers of Jesus).

Based on the order of Jesus' mandates, we can conclude that biblical baptism is to occur after biblical salvation!

Now that we answered the question of "when," let's examine the question of "how." When we consult basic Bible study tools for the definition of the transliterated Greek word "Baptiso" that translates to the English word "baptize," we find the following definitions.

1. To dip repeatedly, to immerse, to submerge (of vessels sunk).
2. To cleanse by dipping or submerging, to wash, to make clean with water, to wash one's self, bathe.
3. To overwhelm.[5]

These descriptors clearly imply that *biblical baptism should be by submersion*. This implication is collaborated by the most straightforward understandings of Jesus' baptism (Mathews 3:13-17) and early church examples in the book of Acts. (I understand there may be unusual situations where submersion is impractical or impossible, but I strongly suggest that any other type of baptism should be an exception to the rule.)

Now that we have answered questions about the "when" and "how" of biblical baptism, let's attempt to determine its meaning. This is more difficult, but it helps to understand that when we examine the whole of scripture, we find that "being baptized" is consistently used symbolically. A comprehensive expounding of this topic is beyond the scope of this book, but let's examine one reference to illustrate the point.

> Do you not know that all of us who have been *baptized into Christ Jesus* were baptized into his death? We were buried therefore with him by baptism into death, in order that, just as Christ was raised from the dead by the glory of the Father, we too might walk in newness of life.
>
> Romans 6:3-4 (emphasis added)

---

[5] (Smith, Greek Lexicon entry for Baptizo 1999)

As we contemplate this scripture, it may seem confusing. How should we understand "baptized into Christ Jesus?" To do this, let's return to the book's previous descriptions of biblical salvation. From these descriptions, we can glean that the salvation event can be succinctly described as leaving an old, spiritually dead life to begin a new, spiritually alive journey as a disciple (follower) of Jesus. With this understanding, the referenced passage becomes much clearer. It is simply describing "all of us" who have experienced biblical salvation.

Now, based on this understanding, we can logically conclude that *physical baptism is symbolic (a picture) of our salvation experience that has already occurred*! It symbolizes our being "buried therefore with him (Jesus) by baptism into death, in order that, just as Christ was raised from the dead by the glory of the Father, we too might walk in newness of life." Further, referring to its basic definition, *it is symbolic of the cleansing (forgiveness of sin) that we experienced at our salvation*. Finally, we can also conclude that since it is typically performed in the presence of other people, hopefully including family and friends, *it is a public testimony to our salvation experience*!

My question now is, "Have you experienced biblical baptism?" If your answer is "no" or "I am not sure," why let this issue be a stumbling block on your spiritual journey? Why not just go ahead and do it? This action brings peace that you have done what Jesus your Lord mandated, and it will give you an opportunity to publicly testify about your salvation experience to those you deeply care about.

I didn't do this until about ten years ago – after being a genuine follower of Jesus involved in various ministries for over thirty years. As described elsewhere in the book, I responded to a church invitation to become a "Christian" at age 12 and was subsequently baptized a few weeks later. However, I can't objectively date my salvation experience until age 37. As a result of listening to an evangelistic message that concluded with an invitation to receive biblical baptism, I was suddenly confronted with the distinct possibility that I had not experienced it. I thought, "Why should this be an issue that I may one day have to explain to Jesus?" As a result, I responded to the invitation and was baptized again at age 71. I hope you will not wait as long as I did to get things right. Please just do it as soon as you have an opportunity!

JOIN THE BODY OF CHRIST

Now we have to address, for some, a "touchy" subject. Over the years, I have heard all the arguments against church (sometimes characterized as "organized religion"), such as, "They just want my money," or "They're just a bunch of hypocrites." I realize these types of accusations are, unfortunately, sometimes true. Churches are always composed of imperfect people. However, it is very difficult, if not impossible, to be all God intends for you to be outside of a church body. Throughout the Bible, we see that God's plan for his people is to participate in family life. As an example, we find the following description of the early church.

> And they devoted themselves to the apostles' teaching and the fellowship, to the breaking of

bread and the prayers. And awe came upon every soul, and many wonders and signs were being done through the apostles. And all who believed were together and had all things in common.

Acts 2:42-44

Here we see God's people living in a loving, family-type relationship. We also see God making himself known in their midst. This is the way the Christian life is supposed to be. If we deviate from it, we suffer consequences. As mentioned previously in the book, you may squeeze into Heaven, but it will be "as through fire." (1 Corinthians 3:15) In that case, you and God's kingdom suffer great loss.

Although many are quick to point out that early followers of Jesus didn't have churches like we have today, which is true. However, modern-day followers of Jesus fulfill four important needs through regular church participation:

- Fellowshipping with Other Jesus-Followers
- Participating in Corporate Worship
- Establishing a Biblical Foundation
- Providing an Outlet for Ministry

We all need loving fellowship with like-minded people. We were created with this need. The need can be simple social interaction, or can involve deep involvements in receiving or providing critical help during life crisis situations. For Jesus followers, these needs can best be met through regular participation in a local church.

As many will argue, it's certainly true that all followers of Jesus can and should worship privately. But there's an added dimension to worship that can only be experienced corporately. This is hard to explain, but when you experience it, you will understand. Please just try it.

In addition to preaching, most church traditions have some type of ongoing Bible study. Typically, the studies are facilitated by inviting a "subject-expert" to lead a Bible conference for the entire congregation, or by gifted teachers in small group settings, either within or outside of the church building. If you are going to mature and be all God intends, you need a strong biblical foundation. Regular participation in church-sponsored Bible study can be a key factor in building this foundation.

All genuine followers of Jesus desire and need an outlet for personal ministry. Based on personal observations over many years, I have found that many who start a spiritual journey, even with biblically correct directions, never discover their calling (gifting) for ministry. Eventually, they become stuck on a spiritual plateau with seemingly no way to proceed. This can lead to serious frustration and spiritual despondency. Depending on calling (gifting), many Jesus followers can avoid this pitfall by finding an outlet for personal ministry within the church they attend. Others find some degree of outlet within the church but supplement it with participation in like-minded parachurch organizations. [The vital importance of finding and exercising your calling (gifting) will be further discussed in a subsequent chapter.]

As was the case for baptism, if you were a professing Christian when you began reading this book, you most likely were already a church member and maybe actively involved in church life. However, as a recently enlightened or new follower of Jesus, you need to reexamine your role within the body of Christ. Are you only filling a "seat," or are you fulfilling the role in God's kingdom that he planned for you?

Perhaps you were a professing Christian before reading this book but not involved in church life – maybe even "turned off" by it. In this case, you may find it difficult to start. Church people are sometimes cliquish and may seem unwelcoming to outsiders. There can also be fear of exposing your limited knowledge of the Bible or church life. However, you need to realize that everyone has to start new adventures somewhere. My strong admonition is to just "buckle up" and begin to experience the Christian life as God designed.

There is an old, often used, illustration about an ember being separated from its fire. Apart from the fire, it cools and eventually loses its glow. Over the years, I have observed this illustration as an apt descriptor for professing Christians who choose, for whatever reason, to separate themselves from the body of Christ.

BEGIN RUNNING TO WIN

With all endeavors in life, it takes effort to succeed. If we are going to succeed in the Christian life, we need to do as the apostle Paul admonishes.

> Do you not know that in a race all the runners run, but only one receives the prize? So run that you may obtain it.
>
> 1 Corinthians 9:24

We shouldn't conclude from this verse that we're in competition with other Jesus followers. It simply means we need to be focused and persistent in doing our best to be all God intends.

Each person's race is unique, but others and I have found two general guidelines to help facilitate a winning race.

Train to Run

In the previous section, we discussed the importance of body life participation. In addition, there are personal disciplines we can practice to help us run in such a way as to win. They can generally be categorized as:

- Daily Quiet Time
- Personal Bible Study
- Spiritual Exercise
- Stewardship Giving

Daily Quiet Time

This discipline requires spending *quality time* with God on a daily basis. Most people find that the best time for doing this is first thing in the morning. Others find their best time is at the end of day. Still others don't have a specific time, but consistently interact with God throughout the day.

When I spend quality time with my wife, or others I care about, we *talk*. (Sometimes my wife has to remind me of the need to do this.) It's the same with God. Talk means two-way communication. Thus, when we communicate with God, we talk (pray) to him and he talks to us, either through his written word, or directly to our spirit.

Because we live in a Judeo-Christian culture, prayer (talking to God) is something we generally understand. It can take different forms but generally falls within four categories.

- Adoration and praise
- Petition (asking God for something we need)
- Thanksgiving (thanking God for something he has done for us or others)
- Intercession (asking God to do something for someone else)

This description of talking to God is probably oversimplified but easily understood by most followers of Jesus.

However, understanding how God talks to us is another story. How can we differentiate God's voice from all others (our thoughts, other people, or demonic sources) vying for our attention? Jesus answered the question this way, "My sheep hear my voice, and I know them, and they follow me." (John 10:27)

This verse is easy for me to understand because of the way I was raised on a Texas ranch. On that ranch, we had all kinds of animals, including cattle, goats, and sheep. In that setting, my father developed a unique "Tarzan" type call. At the time to feed the animals, he walked to a central place where the animals were fed and yelled the call as loud as his voice allowed. Invariably, the animals came running. They had learned to hear his voice. If I or someone else tried to call them, they wouldn't come. I believe this illustrates what Jesus was saying. We learn to hear God's voice by intentionally listening and responding to it!

As mentioned previously, God talks to us either through his written word (the Bible) or directly to our spirit. In both cases, our hearing is expressed by our thoughts.

All actively engaged Jesus followers can readily testify about how God has spoken to them through his written word, but when God (in the person of the Holy Spirit) speaks directly to our spirit, the testimonies become less clear. Yet we are dependent on God speaking to us about many topics not covered in his written word – such as where we are to live, what we do for a living, who we are to marry, and how we are to fulfill our role as ambassadors for God's kingdom. Since God, as a loving Father who knows what is best for us in each of these situations, he certainly wants us to hear from him. But how can we be certain we are hearing God's voice and not some other voice?

As described in a previous chapter, I learned that when I "walk by the Spirit" (Galatians 5:16), I can trust my thoughts. I see this as the Holy Spirit's way of revealing truth and providing guidance for specific situations. The key is being certain I am walking by the Spirit, and of course, I always have to test my thoughts against the truth of scripture.

Maybe you don't understand God's speaking to us in exactly the same way I do, but the point is that we desperately *need* to hear God speaking to us, and we must *learn* to discern his voice. This can only happen by being in a right relationship with him and through an ever persistent, intentional quest to discern his voice (sometimes by a trial-and-error process) from all other voices that may be vying for our attention. This is essential to running our unique race in such a way as to win!

Personal Bible Study

Since God gifts certain people to be "the apostle, the prophets, the evangelist, the shepherds and teachers" (Ephesians 4:11-14), all Jesus followers should carefully listen to these leaders to help them understand fundamental theological truths necessary to enter into and live the Christian life. However, we must always be aware that they are not infallible and can sometimes even be "wolves in sheep clothing." (Mathew 7:15) Therefore, personal knowledge of the basic theological tenets of biblical Christianity is essential. This knowledge allows the Holy Spirit to warn our spirits when we hear something that is theologically questionable or outright wrong.

This routinely happens to me and all genuine followers of Jesus. Sometimes, when exposed to certain preaching or teachings, there comes an immediate sense (a "check") in my spirit that something is not right. I and many other followers of Jesus have learned to trust this check. It requires us to examine scripture to determine if what we are hearing is biblical. Sometimes, we find, surprisingly, that it is, and we have to adjust our theological understanding. Other times we find it is not, and we take whatever steps God directs us. Maybe we express our concern to the person espousing the misinformation, or maybe warn others of the misinformation. Or if the misinformation is serious and persists, maybe we actively confront the issue. However, whatever God directs should always be done in love! Also, we need to be constantly aware that our understanding is not infallible, and we should therefore proceed cautiously with great humility.

The point I am trying to make is that there is no substitute for personal Bible knowledge. *To run a winning race as followers of Jesus, we must be students and not just hearers of God's Word!*

Spiritual Exercise

We all know that intentional and persistent exercise is essential to physical health. The same principle applies to spiritual health. Throughout the Bible, we find examples of people acting in faith. They believed they heard from God and did as they perceived he was directing. Hebrews 11 provides some examples of faith responses to God's perceived direction.

Several years ago, as I pondered these examples, I came to realize that spiritual faith can be thought of as analogous to physical exercise. When we exercise physically, we build physical muscle and become stronger. Similarly, when we exercise faith, we build spiritual muscle and become stronger.

Based on observations over many years, I believe that many within the body of Christ remain spiritually weak because they have not consistently exercised faith. They will readily assert that they will do anything God directs them to do, but since they are never absolutely certain about what he wants, they do little or nothing. But if faith required absolute certainty, it wouldn't be faith. Sometimes exercising faith is scary; it may require venturing to places where we have never been before.

As a follower of Jesus who is continually seeking God's guidance, please don't be afraid to make mistakes. If, to the best of your knowledge, you believe God wants you to do something, just do it! You may find it wasn't really God's voice you heard, and you have to adjust accordingly, but you will find that through the process of exercising faith you are getting stronger. And eventually, as you learn to better hear God's voice, your missteps become much less frequent.

Stewardship Giving

This is a very touchy subject for many within the body of Christ, and for which there isn't universal agreement among biblical scholars or church traditions. However, I will share my viewpoint as a point of reference. You have to decide if it has biblical merit for your personal journey.

The dominant viewpoint within my spiritual tradition, and some others, is that a tithe (generally defined as ten percent of our gross income) should be given to your local church. The theological basis for this viewpoint is based on Old Testament scripture.

> For I the LORD do not change; therefore you, O children of Jacob, are not consumed. From the days of your fathers you have turned aside from my statutes and have not kept them. Return to me, and I will return to you,' says the LORD of hosts. But you say, 'How shall we return?' Will man rob God? Yet you are robbing me. But you say, 'How have we robbed you?' In your tithes and contributions. You are cursed with a curse, for you are robbing me, the whole nation of you. Bring the full tithe into the storehouse, that there may be food in my house. And thereby put me to the test, says the LORD of hosts, if I

will not open the windows of heaven for you and pour down for you a blessing until there is no more need. I will rebuke the devourer for you, so that it will not destroy the fruits of your soil, and your vine in the field shall not fail to bear, says the LORD of hosts. Then all nations will call you blessed, for you will be a land of delight, says the LORD of hosts.

Malachi 3:6-12

To justify this viewpoint, adherents equate "the storehouse" with the local church. As a young follower of Jesus, I adopted this viewpoint of my church tradition and perceived it as God's "rule" for modern day giving. This led my wife and I to begin giving 10% of our gross income to our local church, which was a huge spiritual step for us (at the time). We both look back on this as a significantly positive step in our spiritual journey.

However, as we matured spiritually, we participated in various parachurch organizations whose missions aligned with our spiritual gifting. Thus, much (and eventually most) of our ministry occurred outside the bounds of our local church. These ministries sometimes required substantial financial resources. Then, as "good stewards" of God's resources, we had to decide how to best allocate his resources. We justified this by understanding God's "storehouse" as much more than a local church. It includes all of his kingdom's coffers.

Based on this experience, I offer the following guidelines for your consideration:

1. For beginning followers of Jesus, a tithe to your local church is a very worthy goal, and I believe you and others will be greatly blessed when you make a firm commitment to do it.

2. If most of your ministry is within your local church, then any resources you allocate for outside ministries should probably be beyond your tithe.

3. If most of your ministry is outside your local church, you will have to decide, based on God's leading, how to best allocate the resources he has provided.

The bottom line is that I no longer see a tithe to your local church as a "rule" for New Testament giving. I think we should give as we can best determine from God's leading, which most likely will include substantial financial support to our local church. However, I believe we should regularly and freely seek God's leading about how he would have us allocate the financial resources he has provided. But also, regardless of how he leads, our total giving for both church and outside ministries will, in general, exceed the Old Testament "tithes and contributions" requirement. Based on this viewpoint, even though I don't purposely aim for a tithe, I invariably find that when I examine our year's end income tax return, our total giving has exceeded ten percent of our gross income. I believe if you adopt the above guidelines, you will find the same.

Engage With Running Mate(s)

As briefly mentioned previously in the book, I found two "running mates" early in my spiritual journey. (Some modern-day preachers and teachers use the term "accountability partners" to describe these "running mates.") There have been others along the way, but I trace my most explosive spiritual growth to that early period of my spiritual journey. Our "running" together consisted of meeting in different venues on a weekly basis to share what God was teaching us and what we were doing in response to his teaching. Prayer for ourselves and others we cared about was a consistent component of our sharing. As a result, we ended up as lifelong friends, one of which is still alive, lives down the street from me, and with whom I regularly interact. (I also maintained an ongoing relationship with the other running mate until he went to be with his Lord a few years ago.)

As a follower of Jesus, you will naturally desire to find and spend time with other brothers or sisters in Christ. I have observed that this happens more naturally for women, but for some men, depending on personality and family backgrounds, it is much harder. Regardless of being easy or hard, I strongly encourage you to make the effort necessary to fulfill this need in your life. It is essential to your spiritual health and vitality! Without it, you will have difficulty running in such a way as to win.

Chapter 10
Two Rivers to Cross

The Old Testament is a rich historical account of God's chosen people and how he dealt with them at various times and in specific situations. As such, it contains many types and shadows of spiritual truths that are more fully revealed in the New Testament.

During the past forty-plus years as a follower of Jesus, I have read and heard much about the Exodus part of the Israelite's history as being a type of present-day salvation. However, what about the rest of the Israelite history? Does it also represent types and shadows of present-day spiritual life?

OLD TESTAMENT BACKGROUND

Long ago, God spoke to Moses from the burning bush.

> Then the Lord said, "I have surely seen the affliction of my people who are in Egypt and have heard their cry because of their taskmasters. I know their sufferings, and I have come down to deliver them out of the hand of the Egyptians and to bring them up out of that land to a good and broad land, a land flowing with milk and honey.
>
> Exodus 3:7-8

Note that God's intention was twofold: 1) to deliver his people out of bondage in Egypt, and 2) to bring them into the Promised Land.

As we read the story in Exodus, we find that God's intention to bring his people out of bondage was accomplished when they crossed the Red Sea. However, his intention to bring them into the Promised Land was not immediately realized. Except for Joshua and Caleb, a whole generation of people (those who were 20 years and older who left Egypt) wandered for forty years and eventually died in the wilderness.

The following generations, led by Joshua, finally entered the Promised Land. Under Joshua's leadership, God's plan for his people, as originally given to Moses, was fully accomplished. At the end of the book of Joshua, we see a victorious people living at peace in the land God promised them.

However, after Joshua's death and until the end of the Old Testament, the people as a whole did not demonstrate commitment to pursuing God's plan. There was always a remnant that remained true to him, but most of the people did not. They drifted in and out of spiritual apostasy and ended up in subjection to conquering nations. The ending of the Old Testament is not pretty. Some of God's chosen people remained faithful to God's plan, but most did not. As a result, their identity and spiritual life, as a nation, was only a shell of what it had been.

So what does all of this mean? Does it have an application for today's Jesus follower?

TODAY'S APPLICATION

As previously mentioned, the Old Testament contains many types and shadows of spiritual truths that are more fully revealed in the New Testament. I have come to believe that the whole recorded history of God's chosen people is intended to teach us about present day spiritual life. This belief leads to an understanding that spiritual life can be described as having three basic attributes.

A Coming Out

Biblical commentators typically present the Exodus story as a type of present-day salvation. They see Egypt as a type of the world system, Pharaoh as a type of Satan, slavery as a type of sin's bondage, Moses as a type of Christ, and the Passover lamb as a type of Jesus' sacrificial death. Thus, biblical salvation is equated to God's chosen people being delivered from the present world system that Satan rules and set free from bondage to sin through the intermediary of Jesus' death on the cross.

However, what about the rest of the story? What about the part of the story where all the people who left Egypt, aged twenty and older, except for Joshua and Caleb, died in the wilderness?

To answer this question, let's look at how the New Testament describes these people.

> Therefore I (God speaking) was provoked with that generation, and said, 'They always go astray in their heart; they have not known my ways.' As I swore in my wrath, 'They shall not

enter my rest.'
Hebrews 3:10-11(parentheses added for clarity)

For who were those who heard and yet rebelled? Was it not all those who left Egypt led by Moses? And with whom was he provoked for forty years? Was it not with those who sinned, whose bodies fell in the wilderness? And to whom did he swear that they would not enter his rest, but to those who were disobedient? So, we see that they were unable to enter because of unbelief.

Hebrews 3:16-19

Here we learn that the people who came out of Egypt and died in the wilderness did not enter God's "rest." God's rest was waiting for them in the Promised Land. However, there were enemies in the Promised Land. The people were afraid. They didn't fully believe God and trust his sufficiency to overcome their enemies. Thus, they didn't enter and occupy the land God promised them. *They came out, but didn't enter into*!

Within this context, we are strongly admonished not to be like these Israelites.

Therefore, as the Holy Spirit says, "Today, if you hear his voice, do not harden your hearts as in the rebellion, on the day of testing in the wilderness, where your fathers put me to the test and saw my works for forty years. Therefore I was provoked with that generation, and said, 'They always go astray in their heart; they have not known my ways.' As I swore in my wrath, 'They shall not enter my rest.'"

Hebrews 3:7-11

Take care, brothers, lest there be in any of you an evil, unbelieving heart, leading you to fall away from the living God. But exhort one another every day, as long as it is called "today," that none of you may be hardened by the deceitfulness of sin. For we have come to share in Christ, if indeed we hold our original confidence firm to the end.

Hebrews 3:12-14

The clear implication of these scripture passages is that we have a propensity to be like the Israelites who died in the wilderness. Therefore, we must be diligent not to allow our hearts to be hardened by sin or unbelief.

To summarize, I believe the Israelites who died in the wilderness can be understood as "rocky ground" in Jesus' Parable of the Sower. (Matthew 13:20-21) They showed signs of spiritual life, but when things got tough, they did not have sufficient roots to support life and therefore died. As present-day followers of Jesus, we must not be like these people!

An Entering Into

As the Exodus story unfolds, we see the next generation of Israelites finally entering the Promised Land. Under Joshua's leadership, they believed and trusted God's sufficiency to overcome their enemies as he promised.

Toward the end of the book of Joshua, we find the following account.

> Thus the Lord gave to Israel all the land that he swore to give to their fathers. And they took possession of it, and they settled there. And *the Lord gave them rest* on every side just as he had sworn to their fathers. Not one of all their enemies had withstood them, for the Lord had given all their enemies into their hands. Not one word of all the good promises that the Lord had made to the house of Israel had failed; all came to pass.
>
> Joshua 21:43-45 (emphasis added)

Thus, we see, in contrast to those who died in the wilderness, the next generation of Israelites entered the Promised Land and thereby experienced God's rest. Does this experience have present-day application?

To answer this question, let's continue in the book of Hebrews.

> Therefore, while the promise of entering his (God's) rest still stands, let us fear lest any of you should seem to have failed to reach it. For good news came to us just as it did to them (those who died in the wilderness), but the message they heard did not benefit them, because they were not united by faith with those

who listened.

Hebrews 4:1-2 (parentheses added for clarity)

So then, there remains a Sabbath rest for the people of God, for whoever has entered God's rest has also rested from his works as God did from his.

Hebrews 4:9-10

In these verses, we are told that God's promise of rest still stands today. However, it is not a physical rest like the Israelites experienced in the Promised Land. That was only a type of the spiritual rest God has for today's chosen people. This spiritual rest is what Jesus was talking about when he said, "Come to me, all who labor and are heavy laden, and I will give you rest." (Matthew 11:28)

We can further understand from the above Hebrews passage that we enter God's rest through faith. It's not a onetime decision. It's spiritual life as God designed for us to live. It is a life of great rewards (a Promised Land). However, there are enemies to conquer and lands to occupy. This can only be accomplished by resting from our work and trusting (having faith in) God's sufficiency. Only then can we conquer our enemies and occupy the "land' God desires for us to have.

To summarize, I believe the Israelites who entered the Promised Land can be understood as "good soil" in Jesus' Parable of the Sower. (Mathews 13:23) The fruit of their faith was victory over their enemies and rest in the land God promised them. As present-day followers of Jesus, we too must enter God's rest in the land he uniquely designed for each of us to occupy. Only then can we live victorious and fruitful lives!

Persevering

After Joshua's death, the Israelites continued to live in the Promised Land. As previously mentioned, there was always a remnant that remained true to God, but the nation as a whole began a long history of spiritual decline. Those who remained true persevered in their faith and continued to be a type of "good soil" for present-day Jesus-followers. The others clearly did not persevere.

I believe those who didn't persevere can be understood as thorn-infested ground in Jesus' Parable of the Sower. Their spiritual life was choked by "the cares of the world and the deceitfulness of riches." (Matthew 13:22)

As present-day followers of Jesus, we must be like the Israelite remnant that remained true to God. We must not be like those whose spiritual lives were choked by desires for other things.

SUMMARY

Based on the Old Testament analogies discussed above, we can understand that there are three distinct phases of a successful spiritual journey: 1) a coming out, 2) an entering into, and 3) persevering.

At this point, I am assuming you have clearly come out of your old life. You have experienced biblical salvation either prior to or as a result of reading this book. But you still must enter into the new life God planned for you. When you do this, you will be on track toward God's planned destination as a follower of Jesus. You have entered God's rest! But, you must still "run with endurance the race that is set before us." (Hebrews 12:1) In doing this, God promises that you will "have life and have it abundantly" on this Earth and reap the full benefits of eternal life in Heaven as "heirs of God and fellow heirs with Christ." (John 10:10 and Romans 8:17)

Chapter 11
Proceeding to the Destination

Some years ago, I heard evangelist Bill Glass, whom I greatly admire, talk about how the spiritual life God planned for us is analogous to mountain climbing. The thing I remember most about Bill's message was how he repeatedly used "pitons" to explain how progress is made in spiritual life.

For the non-mountain climber, pitons are metal spikes, firmly driven into rock crevices as a climber ascends a mountain. The blunt end of pitons has an eye through which a rope can be passed. When a piton is firmly secured in a rock crevice and a climber's rope is passed through its eye, it prevents the climber from falling below the level of the piton. Thus, a climber's progress up the mountain is secured as he sequentially places pitons at increasingly higher levels.

THE MOUNTAIN

The objective of mountain climbing is to get to the peak. Some followers of Jesus have never had a clear view of the mountain peak God desires for them to reach. Without a clear view of the peak, they aimlessly attempt to climb the mountain. Eventually, they become frustrated to the point that they resign themselves to camping out on a lower-level ledge of the mountain for the duration of their spiritual journey.

Previously, we discussed God's planned destination for

those who belong to him. We learned that this destination is "to be conformed to the image of his Son." (Romans 8:29) This is the mountain peak we are climbing toward.

Even when presented with a clear view of the mountain peak, some followers of Jesus can't imagine the possibility of getting there. It seems far too lofty for the average climber to achieve. It's true that the most strenuous human efforts will not suffice, but remember – "with God all things are possible." (Matthew 19:26) As previously explained, all those who experienced biblical salvation have a personal guide, the Holy Spirit, who is fully capable of helping them reach the mountain peak.

If ***becoming like Jesus is the mountain peak***, how do we get there?

CLIMBING THE MOUNTAIN

First, the mountain peak is accessible to all climbers. However, we can't climb it in our own strength. To successfully climb it, we must fully comprehend and embrace biblical admonitions such as "God, the Lord, is my strength; he makes my feet like the deer's; he makes me tread on my high places." (Habakkuk 3:19)

Second, although the mountain may be approached from many different backgrounds (life situations, etc.), there is only one pathway to begin climbing the mountain. The Bible described this pathway as, "For the gate is narrow and the way is hard that leads to life, and those who find it are few." (Matthew 7:14) "Life" in this verse is synonymous with salvation described in a previous chapter. It is the first piton in climbing the mountain. (At this point, I assume the reader has firmly secured this piton.)

Third, as we climb, we need to focus continually on our goal, which is to reach the mountain peak. Any lesser goal is not consistent with the life God desires us to live.

Finally, as we progress toward the mountain peak, many pitons will be required. Some of these pitons will be unique to the climber. Others are common to all climbers. Some common pitons (not necessarily in sequential order) include:

- Obedience in Baptism
- Active Participation in the Body of Christ
- Overcoming Sin Strongholds
- A Continual Deepening Relationship with God
  - Relating to God as Father
  - Submission to Jesus as Lord
  - Dependence on the Holy Spirit
- Identification of Spiritual Gifting
- Acceptance of Responsibility to Exercise Gifting as a Servant of God
- Persevering in Faith

Volumes can and have been written about other pitons that may be required to successfully climb the mountain. It suffices to say that climbing the mountain is an all-consuming life adventure. I found that it's the only life journey that fulfills our deepest longings for meaning and purpose. It's what this life is all about. If we miss it, we miss God's plan for our existence.

My hope and prayer are that you have begun climbing the mountain with full intentions of reaching the peak. As you climb, please remember, as a follower of Jesus, you are what the Bible describes as a saint (one who has been set aside for God's purpose). As you progress up the mountain, you will find yourself beginning to function as a servant of God, just as Jesus was. Thus, you will progressively be "conformed to the image of his Son" and therefore fulfill God's ultimate purpose for your life. If you do this, I am confident you will have an exciting and adventurous journey with no regrets!

Chapter 12
Living Free

Based on personal experience and observations over the past forty-plus years, I have come to understand that many Jesus-followers are captives to recurring sin patterns, herein referred to as "sin strongholds." As captives, we are like puppets. When a particular string is pulled, we immediately respond with destructive thoughts or behaviors.

I see Jesus describing this condition when he said, "Truly, truly, I say to you, everyone who practices sin is a slave to sin." (John 8:34) As such, we aren't free to live as God intends.

UNDERSTAND SIN STRONGHOLDS

In order to live in freedom as God intends, there are several things we need to understand about sin strongholds.

We Are Responsible

First, we need to understand that regardless of how the trap was set, we will be held captive if we take the bait. We can't blame our captivity on anything or anyone other than ourselves; *we alone are responsible*! We are responsible for: 1) allowing ourselves to be trapped in the first place, and 2) allowing ourselves to be kept in captivity.

We also need to understand that, as long as we allow ourselves to remain captive, we will be spiritually dysfunctional and thereby unable to completely fulfill the purpose God created us for.

Captivity is Not Normal

Next, we need to understand that remaining in captivity is not the normal Christian life. I have talked to many Jesus-followers, some in places of leadership, who honestly believe we are destined to a life of defeat. In essence, their attitude is, "I am just a rotten sinner and that's all I will ever be." (I will fully address this type of attitude and how it is sometimes rationalized in a subsequent chapter.)

Yes, we are sinners and will always "fall short of the glory of God." (Romans 3:23) However, as followers of Jesus, we should, as repeatedly expounded throughout this book, continually becoming more like him. As such, we should increasingly be engaged in the process of overcoming sin. If we don't, there are serious implications. Please consider the following passage.

> Little children, let no one deceive you. Whoever practices righteousness is righteous, as he is righteous Whoever makes a practice of sinning is of the devil, for the devil has been sinning from the beginning.... No one born of God makes a practice of sinning, for God's seed abides in him; and he cannot keep on sinning, because he has been born of God.
>
> 1 John 3:7-9

This scripture clearly reveals that, as followers of Jesus, God doesn't intend for us to live as captives to sin strongholds, and if we do, there is reason to question the validity of our relationship with God.

We Can Be Set Free

Finally, we need to understand that our situation is not hopeless. After Jesus said, as referenced above, *"everyone who practices sin is a slave to sin,"* he followed with the statement *"So if the Son sets you free, you will be free indeed."* (John 8:36, emphasis added)

Thus, it's clear from scripture that we can be set free from sin's captivity (from being a "slave to sin"), but we need to understand the biblical process through which this can happen. As we examine scripture, we find there is only *one process* to overcome sin strongholds. This process is *repentance*!

In Revelation 2-3, Jesus commanded his followers in the early churches to "repent" of particular sins. In each case, he followed his command with the statement "one who conquers." These admonitions clearly reveal the close association between "repentance" and "overcoming."

UNDERSTAND REPENTANCE

As stated above, the biblical process for overcoming sin strongholds is repentance. However, many people, including some Jesus-followers, don't have a clear understanding of repentance. They understand it as being sorry for what they have done and asking for forgiveness. Some Jesus-followers ask for forgiveness over and over again but remain captive to sin strongholds. Some try to overcome these strongholds through human self-help efforts, but these approaches don't produce lasting results. Sin strongholds are spiritual in nature and therefore can only be overcome through a spiritual process. The Bible describes this process as follows.

> For Godly grief produces a repentance that leads to salvation without regret, whereas worldly grief produces death.
>
> 2 Corinthians 7:10

This passage makes it clear that the spiritual root of repentance is a "godly grief." It is much deeper than "worldly grief." Godly grief is the result of a deep conviction, brought about by the Holy Spirit that we have offended Holy God. Sometimes worldly grief produces regrets or guilt feelings that lead us to ask forgiveness, but it doesn't result in any fundamental transformation of our lives. In contrast, true repentance results in a transformed life.

My simple understanding of the process of repentance can be summarized as follows:

- Initiated by the Holy Spirit
- Results in godly grief
- Leads to a *change of mind*
- Results in a change of direction

This is the only process God provided for Jesus-followers to be set free from sin strongholds.

SUMMARY

This chapter explained that biblical repentance is the only process to overcome sin strongholds. Your stronghold(s) may be different than mine, but please consider how they are hindering your relationship with God and keeping you from fulfilling all he desires for your life. My hope and prayer are that the Holy Spirit uses the simple process described in this chapter to set you free from any sin strongholds that may exist in your life.

PERSONAL NOTE

Many of my sin strongholds were identified and overcome almost immediately after my life-changing, adult encounter with God, as described throughout this book. However, as I have matured somewhat as a follower of Jesus, the Holy Spirit, from time to time, made me aware of strongholds that were previously unknown.

For example, in recent years, the Holy Spirit made me aware of an ongoing, deeply embedded anger that caused me to be and do less than God planned for me. I don't know the origin of this stronghold. Maybe there were some childhood experiences it could be traced to, or maybe it had a demonic origin. I really don't know. However, throughout my adult life, I can remember responding to certain actions by other people with explosive anger. Although this could happen with anyone, it most often occurred with those I loved most – my wife or children. Although I was somewhat sensitized to the problem and tried to keep it under control, it was always there, simmering and waiting for the right set of circumstances to initiate an explosive response. When it happened, I immediately recognized it was wrong, and typically asked God and the other person involved for forgiveness. Since I had seemingly gotten over the episode and asked for forgiveness, I assumed (incorrectly) that the other person involved had also gotten over it. However, I was leaving a long trail of relationship wreckage behind me without realizing it.

Several years ago, I was participating in a men's study at the church where my wife and I attend. As part of the study, my assignment was to ask someone who knew me well to grade my maturity level for particular spiritual attributes. Since the person who knows me best is my wife of sixty-plus years, I asked her to do the evaluation. Well, you would have to know my wife to fully understand, but believe me – she doesn't grade on any type of curve. I understood this, so on a scale of zero to five (zero being "terrible" and five being "excellent"), I wasn't expecting to get all fives, but I was expecting to do fairly well.

As I read her evaluation, I was getting some threes, fours, and sometimes even a five, which is about what I anticipated. However, when I got to her assessment of my "anger," I was shocked to see a *zero*.

A *zero*? How could this be? I was totally mortified! How could I be my Father's son and be graded a zero? It was as if I had been stabbed in the heart with a dagger.

When I questioned my wife about why she had given me a zero grade, she reminded me about all the times my explosive anger damaged my relationship with her and especially with our children.

After the initial shock, I experienced a deep sense of remorse. For the first time, I acknowledged that my anger was a serious sin stronghold, offensive to God and others. Over the next several hours, I faced what I now understand as "godly grief," not only for what I had done, but for who I allowed myself to become. I realized I could not really call myself a follower of Jesus and allow this stronghold to remain in my life. I came to a deep realization that my relationship with God and other people was more important than the sin I allowed to hold me captive.

Finally, I fell on my knees before God and asked him not only to forgive me but also to help me never express explosive anger again, as long as I live. Later, sitting at the feet of my wife, I did the same thing with her.

I wish I could tell you this stronghold has been completely overcome. I can honestly say its occurrence and severity have greatly diminished, but there are still times when something triggers it. When this happens, I have learned to immediately call upon Jesus for help. When I do this, the angry feelings subside, and I can deal with the situation more rationally.

While, I realize that the potential of this stronghold raising its ugly head is something I may deal with for the rest of my life, I also know that through the process of repentance, and with the Holy Spirit's help, I *can* prevail in overcoming it.

If my family, or anyone else who might have been on the receiving end of my anger ever reads this book, please know I am deeply sorry for any wounds I caused. I know my anger was sin, and I hope you find it in your hearts to forgive me.

And, most of all, I pray that my sin stronghold will not hinder you from living the life God planned for you.

Chapter 13
Surviving Storms

Years ago, I attended a church service in which people were testifying about various struggles (herein referred to as "storms") they were facing in life.

One man stood up and said something to the effect of, "Since becoming a Christian, I have never experienced a storm of any kind."

I had no way to evaluate the credibility of his statement, but my immediate thought was, "If you haven't experienced one yet, you will."

It also seemed like he was mimicking Job's "friends" in being judgmental of those who were experiencing storms. After forty-plus years as an active follower of Jesus, my thoughts haven't changed.

Due to major societal changes in the U.S. where I live, compounded by my increasing age and that of my contemporaries, I am seeing ever-increasing storms everywhere I look. Because of the direct impact they are having on family members, and others I deeply care about, I have become increasingly sensitive to these storms.

This chapter describes storms followers of Jesus may face in life and how we can best survive them.

WHY GOD ALLOWS STORMS

Before we attempt to understand storms of life, we need to address the obvious question, "Why does God allow them in his creation, and especially in the lives of those who belong to him?" Answers to this question have been postulated by theologians throughout recorded Christian history.

However, for me a simple answer is sufficient. God created humanity with free will. As such, we are responsible for our actions and therefore reap what we sow. Thus, our actions, or inactions, that are contrary to God's created order cause storms in God's good creation. Except for some God-orchestrated storms and Satan-orchestrated storms, discussed later in this chapter, we are the storm-causers!

Based on this understanding, let's now explore storms that can occur in the lives of Jesus-followers and how we can best survive them.

JESUS-FOLLOWER STORMS

As will be described, some storms in the lives of Jesus-followers are inevitable. They can be categorized as follows.

General Storms

These are storms that happen to all people because we live in a fallen world. When Adam and Eve rebelled against God's direct command, they suffered his righteous judgement. Having free wills, they chose to live independent of God's loving provision and reaped what they sowed. As Adam and Eve's descendants, all humanity, in one way or another, has chosen the same path.

All the problems in the world (war, injustice, poverty, crime, etc.) can be traced to humanity's choices. When we understand this, we can't blame God for storms we may experience. We can only blame ourselves and our fellow humans.

In some cases, God may intervene in these types of storms. Many Jesus-followers can testify about specific instances of God's intervention, generally in response to prayer. And sometimes, storms of this type can be mitigated by avoiding circumstances that create them. However, most of the time we are stuck with weathering them with the comfort and aid of the Holy Spirit.

Self-Induced Storms

These are storms that result from specific things we do or don't do. As previously mentioned, we reap what we sow. In these cases, the resulting storms have been self-induced.

For example, if I drink alcohol or abuse drugs in ways that result in a car wreck, I may seriously hurt myself or someone else and likely face legal consequences. Similarly, consistent overeating eventually leads to serious health problems and probably a shortened lifespan.

There are many other examples I could point to. However, the point is that many storms we face in life are self-induced.

Upon becoming Jesus-followers, we are forgiven and born again (born of God) to live new lives but are still subject to consequences of our previous life. However, the good news is that self-induced storms resulting from our past can be mitigated, and future storms of this type are preventable. We simply have to begin living the way God's grace empowers us to live!

Satan-Orchestrated Storms

Satan-orchestrated storms fall within two categories.

Storms to Defeat

These are storms orchestrated by Satan to deceive and thus defeat Jesus-followers. He does this by setting traps. In setting these traps, he uses bait that appeals to our natural fleshly desires. He disguises the bait by making it seem innocent or even good. He did this with Adam and Eve, and he does it with us.

The U.S. entertainment industry is the best example I can think of. Satan consistently uses this industry to picture lifestyles contrary to God's created order for life. When we adopt these lifestyles, we get caught in Satan's trap and suffer consequences as a result.

There are many more examples I could point to. However, the point is that many of the storms we face in life are a result of *allowing ourselves* to get caught in Satan's traps.

The way to prevent these storms is to be ever aware of Satan's strategies and to avoid taking his bait. This may require major relationship and lifestyle changes that avoid exposure to his bait.

Storms to Destroy

Jesus-followers have faced persecution storms throughout Christian history. They are designed to diminish God's witness to a lost and dying world. Satan instigates these storms through people and institutions he controls.

The basis for present-day persecution varies depending on where we reside. In some parts of the world, Satan uses the same approach he used in Jesus' day. He uses dominant religious institutions to suppress, ostracize, imprison, or even martyr followers of Jesus.

In other parts of the world, core Christian beliefs and values clash with established government institutions. In such societies, Satan uses government institutions to persecute Jesus-followers.

Because of our Judeo-Christian heritage, Jesus-followers who are privileged to live in the U.S. have been largely isolated from persecution storms. However, in my lifetime, I am seeing core Christian beliefs and values become increasingly challenged by counterculture. Social issues like same-sex marriage and homosexual or transgender practices are beginning to fuel hostility toward Jesus-followers whose faith demands they take a stand against such practices. It is easy to imagine a future in which Jesus-followers in the U.S. will face increasing hostility and more severe forms of persecution.

As Jesus-followers we should not be surprised by persecution storms since he warned that the same things that happened to him would happen to his followers. (1 Peter 4:12-16) Thus, as true followers of Jesus, these storms are inevitable. However, scripture promises that the rewards for not compromising our faith far outweigh the costs. (Luke 6:22-23)

God-Orchestrated Storms

God-orchestrated storms fall within three categories.

Testing

Abraham's commanded sacrifice of Isaac and Jesus' wilderness experience are prime examples of this type of storm.

In scripture, we are told, "Count it all joy, my brothers, when you meet trials of various kinds, for you know that the testing of your faith produces steadfastness." (James 1:2-3) This passage doesn't say *"if"* it says *"when"* you meet trials. Thus, all Jesus-followers should anticipate sometimes stormy trials that test our faith.

When God orchestrates or allows testing in our lives, we must remember it is always for our good. As such, we should embrace it as evidence that God loves and wants the best for us.

Discipline

Discipline is similar to testing, except it is in response to some specific wrong we have done.

As Jesus-followers, the Holy Spirit always convicts when we wander outside the boundaries of God's created order. Our response should be to immediately repent. However, if we don't, God may orchestrate some type of storm to get our attention. Hopefully, this leads to repentance and reconciliation.

It is important to remember that when God disciplines us, he is treating us "as sons." (Hebrews 12:7) Since God loves those that belong to him, we can be assured his discipline is always for our good. Therefore, our goal should be to learn from these types of storms and respond quickly with repentance!

Judgement

God's judgement is a next step beyond discipline. If we persist in disobedience or rebellion, and won't respond to conviction or discipline, God's judgement will eventually fall, even upon those who belong to him.

The Israelites, who were delivered from Egyptian captivity, but ended up dying in the wilderness, are a prime example of this judgement. (Hebrews 3:7-19) The death of Ananias and Sapphira is another example. (Acts 5:1-10) Present-day Jesus-followers should also seriously consider the possibility of God's judgement for those who somehow disrespect the Lord's Supper. (1 Corinthians 11:17-34)

These, and many other examples throughout scripture, should provide ample warning that Jesus-followers are not exempt from God's judgement when they persistently disobey or rebel against him. God's basic nature demands this righteous judgement.

SURVIVE UNPREVENTABLE STORMS

As previously discussed, some storms that Jesus-followers face are preventable. However, others aren't!

Our response to unpreventable storms is a measure of our trust in God. It is important to understand that Satan who will do everything possible to weaken or destroy this trust. One of his primary strategies is to use unpreventable storms to sow seeds of doubt about God's goodness. We must be careful not to fall for this ploy.

Of all the biblical illustrations about how Jesus-followers should react to unpreventable storms, the story of Joseph (Genesis 37 and 39-48) probably provides the best insight. Joseph suffered unpreventable storms throughout his lifetime:

1. He was ostracized and placed in physical danger by his brothers.
2. He was forcibly enslaved.
3. He was falsely accused and imprisoned.

And yet, his trust in God never wavered! As a result, he eventually realized the life dream that God had given him as a youth.

If we persevere in our trust, we may never see the full extent of our dreams in this life, but we will in eternity. As followers of Jesus, we must persevere in our trust of God's goodness. This is our only option!

Chapter 14
All is Not Vanity

Recently, I have been thinking about how we should spend our time as followers and servants of Jesus. Most of us have leisure time we can spend as we desire. This is especially true during retirement years.

When I read about the early church, it's hard to find examples of leisure time. But there are numerous biblical guidelines for how we should spend our time in general. I think these guidelines can be summarized by this verse.

> Look carefully then how you walk, not as unwise but as wise, making the best use of the time, because the days are evil.
>
> Ephesians 5:15-16

In this chapter, I will use three scenes from my life to illustrate this guideline.

SCENE 1

During a recent morning, I found myself sitting on the back patio of our home observing typical nature drama I often see there. Some years ago, my wife and I retired from a bustling metropolis setting to a peaceful golfing community. Our home backs up to the seventeenth fairway of our country club golf course. In addition to the golf course, we have eight mature pecan trees plus other smaller trees and bushes in our yard that provide a beautiful setting for our home.

The pecan trees are arranged so there is a small hole in the tree canopy directly above where I normally sit on our patio. Sometimes, the hole seems like a portal through which I can intimately communicate with God.

On that particular morning, a lot was going on. A constant parade of golfers teed off on the fairway directly in front of where I was sitting. As they went through their synchronized routines in typical golfing attire, they looked like little tin soldiers marching off to war.

A juvenile squirrel performed spectacular, seemingly death-defying antics among the branches of our pecan trees. Sometimes, it stopped and look at me as if wondering, "What kind of strange creature have I encountered?"

In addition, various types of beautifully arrayed small birds fluttered here and there among the trees and bushes, and one lone buzzard flew high above the trees.

As I observed the scene, everything seemed beautifully peaceful, pleasurably entertaining, and quietly restful. However, in the back of my mind, probably caused by my Type A personality, I had nagging questions about wasting my time.

SCENE 2

Later that same day, as I was driving to have lunch with my brother and talk about how to best care for our 100-year-old mother, a different kind of experience occupied my thoughts. This experience occurred the previous Sunday afternoon when my wife and I visited a local juvenile center where youths, aged 10 to 17, were incarcerated for various crimes.

During this visit, we shared the gospel with three girls, probably in the 14 to 16 age range. As we shared with the girls, one of them interrupted to ask a question. She stated that because of her background, she had developed a tendency to same-sex attractions. She wanted to know if she could continue this kind of lifestyle and still have a relationship with God. As gently as we could, my wife and I shared that the continual *practice* of any type of sin is not compatible with being a follower of Jesus.

We then resumed sharing the gospel, concluding with the Romans 10:9 statement, "if you confess with your mouth that Jesus is Lord and believe in you heart that God raised him from the dead, you will be saved." We pointed out that the original Greek word translated "Lord" in this passage can mean owner, master, sovereign (king), or God. So a confession that Jesus is Lord means we are submitting to him as our personal owner, master, king, and God. If he truly is our Lord, we will naturally want to live the way he desires. At this point, I sensed intense spiritual warfare and didn't know how to proceed.

To further complicate the situation, the female guard who accompanied the girls chimed in that she didn't see any problem if same-sex relationships were based on love. She even used 1 Corinthians 13, taken completely out of context, to argue her case.

Finally, in desperation, I confessed to the girls that I didn't know how to proceed. I told them I didn't want them to miss an opportunity to confess Jesus as Lord, but I also didn't want to coerce them into making an insincere decision. I simply asked, "Do any of you believe in your heart that Jesus was resurrected from the dead and want to confess him as your personal Lord?"

To our surprise and delight, the girl who confessed to same-sex attractions responded with a very affirmative yes! It seemed obvious she was clearly choosing Jesus' Lordship over her same-sex attraction. One of the other girls also responded affirmatively. After praying a simple salvation prayer in which both girls confessed Jesus as their personal Lord, we welcomed two newborn Jesus-followers into the family of God.

As we were departing, the female guard commented that we had given her some things to think about.

SCENE 3

Later, in the process of writing the book, I remembered another scene that happened about five to seven years ago. I was on my way to an evangelistic prison event with Bill Glass' Behind the Walls ministry. As I remember, it was a weekend event somewhere in the West Texas area. At the time, I was very actively engaged in my then current hobby (my wife calls them "obsessions"). My goal was to find and collect at least one of every type of vintage marble (yes, those little round things that children used to play with) that had ever been made.

In those days, one of the best places to find old marbles, dating back to the late 1800s, was at antique stores. As I was driving to the event, I came to a small town that had such a store. I pulled into the parking lot just before closing time. When I entered the store, I immediately encountered the store attendant sitting in a wheelchair. She was older, had a downcast demeanor, and obviously had serious health issues. In my spirit, I sensed a strong prompting to talk to her. But I was so focused on my marble-collecting mission that I ignored the prompting, found and bought a few marbles, and went on my way.

As I proceeded on my journey, I sensed an almost audible voice asking, "Are your marbles more important than that lady whom I created and love?" Although I participated in all the prison events during the weekend, I could not turn loose of that question. As a result, I realized I had made a serious spiritual blunder and resolved to stop at the store on my way home and somehow try to make amends.

The prison event was over at about 3:00 PM and the store was at least two hours away. I immediately jumped into my pickup and drove as fast as the speed limit allowed (and maybe even a little faster) to get to the store before its closing time. I pulled into the parking lot almost exactly at 5:00 PM, just as the last customer was leaving. I hurried to the store and entered to find the same lady as I found her before. I went directly to her, explained how God had been speaking to me, profusely apologized, and ended up having a very uplifting spiritual conversation and prayer time with her.

REFLECTIONS

So how do these life scenes relate to the biblical guidelines stated earlier? It's obvious that in Scene 2, I was "making the best use of the time," and that initially in Scene 3, I wasn't. But how about Scene 1?

As discussed earlier in the book, we were created with a

strong propensity to gratify ourselves. This is our earthly human nature. In Scene 1, I was simply doing what came naturally, and it was very self-gratifying! However, was I just wasting my time? In that situation, I was taking a break from something, but I don't remember from what.

Another of my current "obsessions" is playing online chess. If I'm not careful, I can spend hours in this pastime. If I was taking a break from chess, this scene was possibly just a continuation of wasted time. However, I also distinctly remember sensing a very restful and peaceful communion with God as I watched his creation in full panoramic, colorful display. Upon reflection, I can't definitively say whether or not I was "making the best use of the time."

Regardless, the point is that we need to be very careful to keep self-gratification in proper perspective. If we allow our time to be *consumed* by self-gratification, we will miss the purpose of our existence. The end result will be akin to the "vanity of vanities" Solomon expresses in Ecclesiastes 1:2.

But life doesn't have to be like this! In the Bible, we see many examples of ordinary people fulfilling their God-given destiny. I am sure they all experienced times when they enjoyed life in ways that were very self-gratifying. But there were also times when they set self-gratification aside for a greater purpose. In effect, they had to deny themselves to fulfill God's unique purpose for their lives. I see this is what Jesus was describing when he said, "If anyone would come after me, let him deny himself and take up his cross daily and follow me." (Luke 9:23)

Although our lives may never seem as significant as some examples in the Bible, or even as what we see other people doing today, I firmly believe God has a uniquely individualized purpose for each of our lives. We may not have one of the more visible spiritual gifts (I Corinthians 12:12-31), or we may only be a one-talent person (Matthew 25:14-30), but in God's eyes, our purpose has eternal significance. And when we understand and fulfill this purpose, life takes on a completely new, meaningful dimension that is exciting and adventurous. But for this to happen, we must sometimes be willing to deny our natural propensity for self-gratification and be intentional about how we invest our time.

No, all of life does not have to be vanity. *With the Holy Spirit's direction and help, we can fulfill our God-given destiny and make an eternal difference in the world we live in*!

Chapter 15
Completing the Journey

As I progress through the twilight of my life, I have become increasingly resolved to leave this life with no regrets. I certainly have regrets from my earlier life that not only affected me but also other people whom I love deeply. However, I have asked for God's forgiveness and have tried to make amends as best I can. That is all I can do. Those regrets have been resolved to the best of my ability.

If you have not fully dealt with past regrets, I strongly recommend you do so *as soon as possible*! I have known many Jesus-followers over the years who have been trapped in their past. This is a primary tactic of our archenemy Satan. If he can convince us we are somehow unforgivable or irreparably damaged, he has won a major battle. In the end, God will win the war, but our effectiveness in accomplishing his kingdom objectives will be greatly diminished.

How can we best live regret-free from this point forward? This chapter will provide some guidelines I hope will be helpful.

AMBASSADORS

The apostle Paul describes Jesus-followers as "ambassadors for Christ." (2 Corinthians 5:20) We all have a general idea of what ambassadors are. They are designated people appointed to represent their government to other governments.

There are only two spiritual kingdoms, the kingdom of God and the kingdom of Satan. Scripture tells us Satan is the present "ruler of this world." (John 12:31, 14:30, and 16:11) This does not imply that the two kingdoms are equal. Satan is a created being just as you and I are. In absolute contrast, Jesus was not created. (See John 1:1-14 and Philippians 2:5-11.) As God manifested in human form, he is forever "King of kings and Lord of lords." (Revelation 19:16) Thus our designation as an ambassador for Christ is to represent his kingdom to the kingdom of this world.

There is one other important thing we need to understand about ambassadors. To the degree that they carry out the agenda of the governments they represent, they have the full authority and backing of those governments. Similarly, when we are faithful to King Jesus' agenda, we have his full authority and backing.

To fulfill our role as an ambassador for Christ, we must fully understand and embrace the agenda of his kingdom. To effectively do this, we must do the following.

Be Firmly Grounded in God's Word

As previous stated in Chapter 9, we can listen to other Jesus-followers and ingest various types of Christian media that may give us some insights, but our ultimate source for understanding King Jesus' agenda has to be the Bible. Thus, instead of casual readers, we must be students of scripture.

However, we can't stop there. As the apostle James said, Jesus-followers must be "doers of the word, and not hearers only." (James 1:22) We must understand that *desire is not the same as doing*. I see many Jesus-followers who voice a desire to serve God but never quite get around to doing it. They end up somehow rationalizing that desire is sufficient. Thus, from a spiritual perspective, their life is largely wasted. We can't be like that! To be effective ambassadors for Christ, we must follow his teachings and be obedient to his commands.

Function Within the Body of Christ

Also, as previously stated in Chapter 9, we must understand we aren't lone rangers. The apostle Paul describes how all Jesus-followers are gifted to perform unique functions within the body of Christ. (See 1 Corinthians 12.)

Looking back, even to childhood events, I can see that God has been preparing me to fulfill the role of an evangelist. But it wasn't until age 37, through God-orchestrated circumstances that I clearly understood and surrendered to God's calling. It was only then that his gifting became operable in my life. Your gifting may be different from mine, but according to scripture, you have at least one that is uniquely tailored for your planned participation within the body of Christ.

Since our function within the body of Christ is a gift, we must realize we can't take credit for any fruit that results from it. We have to continually remind ourselves that any fruit produced by our gifting is only the result of God working through our lives. Our responsibility is to "abide" in Jesus and let his work flow through us. (John 15:1-5) This understanding helps keep our natural fleshly egos in check!

Also, we must understand that our viewpoint of the Christian life is biased; it is seen through the lens of our gifting. Because of this, we are susceptible to seeing other functions within the body of Christ as not as important as ours. If we allow this attitude to fester, it can cause frustration and an unloving attitude toward other Jesus-followers. We must continually remind ourselves that all functions within the body of Christ are designed by God to accomplish his purpose.

Finally, we must stay focused on our gifting. In the churches I have been involved in, it is very easy to get distracted. It seems as if there are always more needs than people to fulfill them. In my earlier life as a Jesus-follower, I tended to do whatever was asked of me. As a result, I was not as effective within the body of Christ as I could have been. I now realize I must be free to say "no" when asked to fulfill roles outside of my primary gifting. To be as effective as possible within the body of Christ, I suggest you do the same.

Be Credible

To be effective ambassadors, we must be credible! In today's society, we are bombarded daily with news about people who have lost credibility. Their speech or actions are so abhorrent to God's design it is impossible to pay serious attention to them. If my messages as an evangelist are going to be seriously considered, my walk must match my talk! The same principle applies to all giftings.

As I contemplate this, I think about the qualities described in 2 Peter 1:3-11:

- Virtue (moral excellence, goodness, righteousness)
- Knowledge
- Self-Control

- Steadfastness
- Godliness
- Brotherly Affection
- Love

In this passage, the apostle Peter says, "For if these qualities are yours and are increasing, they keep you from being ineffective or unfruitful in the knowledge of our Lord Jesus Christ." (2 Peter 1:8)

Peter's admonitions describe a credible lifestyle we must possess to effectively fulfill our God-given role within the body of Christ.

Be Confident

We must firmly believe the message we are proclaiming, either through words or actions. I have found that people can somehow sense confidence, and it's a major factor in their response.

This became clear during a mission project to one of the Central American countries (I don't remember which one). My interpreter was the associate pastor and apparent heir for the lead pastor role in the church I was working with. We were sharing the gospel in many homes and seeing most of the people make decisions for Christ. At the end of one day's visits, he said, "You really believe what you are sharing, don't you?" At the time, his statement seemed odd to me. But after thinking about it, I concluded that he probably was associating my confidence with the largely positive responses we were witnessing, which I believe was true.

This kind of confidence can only be birthed by the Holy

Spirit as he reveals the truths of scripture. Therefore, as stated earlier, we must be a student of scripture and be confident that the Holy Spirit is clearly leading in whatever God has for us to do. In some cases, I found that subjecting my understanding of scripture to mature peer reviews has bolstered my confidence.

Be Motivate by Love

In studying the gospel records, we see that everything Jesus did during his time on planet Earth was motivated by love. Love is another thing people can sense. If love is sensed, people will be positively impacted. If they don't sense love, they will typically disregard whatever we are attempting to accomplish.

Without love, whatever I proclaim as an evangelist will only be "a noisy gong or a clanging symbol." (I Corinthians 13:1) The same general principle applies to all giftings.

SUMMARY

This chapter has been written as an exhortation about how to live regret-free during the remainder of our time on planet Earth. As described, there are a number of things we must do to accomplish this objective.

In life, I have found that very little is accomplished outside of focused goals. I see so many Jesus-followers who just seem to be wandering through life with little or no comprehension of why God put them on planet Earth.

Is this really the way you want to live? Don't you really want to live regret-free? If so, I encourage you to find out how God gifted you to function within the body of Christ. There are readily available resources to help you discover your gifting. Your church probably has simple tests that can provide clues. Or maybe you can find an answer through simply discussing the subject with someone who knows you well.

But don't stop there! Take steps toward being the ambassador for God's kingdom he equipped you to be. You may want to consider the following prayer that was shared in a Bible study class my wife and I attend.

> *Lord, give me a Kingdom project that will capture my passion, challenge my giftedness, and inspire the investment of my treasure.*

I don't know who originated this prayer, but it is certainly applicable to living a *regret-free* life!

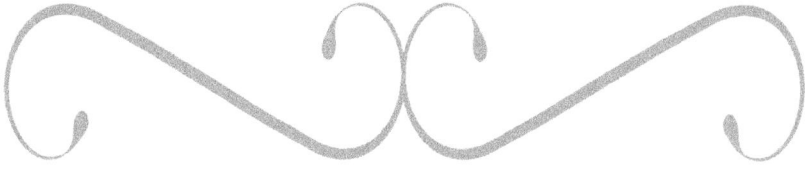

Part 4
Potential Hazards and Diversions

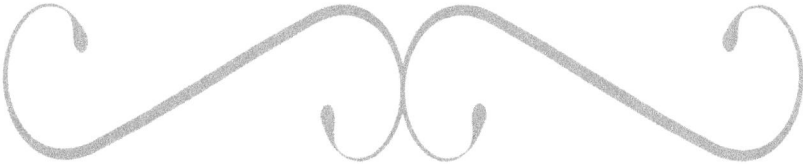

Now that we are proceeding on our journey, we need to be aware of potential hazards and diversions that can hinder or slow our journey to God's planned destination.

Although multiple books have and could be written about the many hazards and diversions that can be encountered during a spiritual journey, this part of the book describes three I have been particularly sensitized to during my personal journey.

Chapter 16
Rationalization of Sin

As I interact with other Jesus-followers, it seems many have given up in their efforts to overcome sin. When I have tried to address the subject with them, I typically get immediate push back. They quickly point to particular scripture passages in an attempt to show that overcoming sin is not practically achievable. I have come to believe they are misapplying these passages to rationalize continuing sin in their lives.

As a result, I believe that misapplication of these passages is a major problem within the body of Christ. Further, I see these misapplications as so strongly entrenched in some Christian traditions that it is considered almost heretical to even question them. Thus, they have a continuing negative impact on how the Christian life is perceived and lived.

MISAPPLIED SCRIPTURE PASSAGES

The scripture passages in question are Romans 7:14-24, 1 Corinthians 3:1-3, and 1 Timothy 1:12-15. It is interesting to note that these passages were all authored by the apostle Paul. Many (maybe most) Jesus-followers would agree that if anyone should be considered a model of how to live the Christian life, it would be Paul. And yet, as we will see, some of his writings are used to rationalize continuing sin in their lives.

Romans 7:14-24 Passage

This scripture passage is, by far, the most often used rationale for continuing sin in the lives of Jesus-followers. It's a fairly long passage, but let's take time to read it.

> For we know that the law is spiritual, but I am of the flesh, sold under sin. For I do not understand my own actions. For I do not do what I want, but I do the very thing I hate. Now if I do what I do not want, I agree with the law, that it is good. So now it is no longer I who do it, but sin that dwells within me. For I know that nothing good dwells in me, that is, in my flesh. For I have the desire to do what is right, but not the ability to carry it out. For I do not do the good I want, but the evil I do not want is what I keep on doing. Now if I do what I do not want, it is no longer I who do it, but sin that dwells within me.
>
> So I find it to be a law that when I want to do right, evil lies close at hand. For I delight in the law of God, in my inner being, but I see in my members another law waging war against the law of my mind and making me captive to the law of sin that dwells in my members. Wretched man that I am! Who will deliver me from this body of death?
>
> Romans 7:14-24

When many Jesus-followers read this passage, they understand that Paul is describing his personal life *as an apostle*. Therefore, they rationalize that, since Paul was apparently in bondage to sin, their own bondage is normal.

This is a viewpoint I have heard preached and taught ever since becoming a follower of Jesus. However, even cursory research will quickly reveal that there has been, and continues to be, serious theological challenges to this viewpoint.

I don't have the theological credentials to resolve all of the controversies surrounding this scriptural passage. However, I will share a few observations about the passage that seem logically persuasive to me.

First, to understand the subject passage, it is important to note that it is inserted between two chapters (Romans 6 and 8), about which there is little, if any, controversy. In Romans 6, Paul clearly states that Jesus-followers should "no longer be enslaved to sin." (Romans 6:6) Later in Romans 8, Paul continues this theme by stating that they "are debtors, not to the flesh, to live according to the flesh." (Romans 8:12) It's therefore logical to conclude that, regardless of what Romans 7:14-24 is trying to communicate, this passage *doesn't* mean that Jesus-followers are: 1) engaged in a spiritual battle with sin that can't be won, or 2) are in a continuous losing battle with sin as the status quo.

These conclusions are strongly supported by the overall tenet of New Testament scripture where Jesus-followers are continually exhorted to live pure and holy lives. Why would this be the case if they were hopelessly destined to live in bondage to sin?

Second, in context, Paul is describing a person who is living under the law. He describes such a person as, "I do not do the good I want, but the evil I do not want is what I keep on doing." (Romans 7:19)

But, as an apostle, Paul was no longer living under the law. Therefore, he couldn't be describing himself in his current state. That being the case, why did he write in first person? I don't have a definitive answer to that question, but can suggest two possibilities.

1. He was describing his previous life as a religious Jew while living under the law.
2. It was simply an artifact of his writing style in describing a generic religious person who was living under the law.

Even if we can't satisfactorily resolve the first-person issue, we still have logical conundrums to deal with. In many scripture passages, Paul described his life as an apostle in ways that are mutually exclusive to the Romans 7 passage. For example, he said, "I have been crucified with Christ. It is no longer I who live, but Christ who lives in me. And the life I now live in the flesh I live by faith in the Son of God, who loved me and gave himself for me." (Galatians 2:20)

How can the person described in this passage be the same person who is described in the Romans 7 passage?

Also, how could Paul instruct others to live pure and holy lives, a major theme in his letters, if he found himself unable to do so?

I Corinthians 3:1-3 Passage

This is another scripture passage that is sometimes used to rationalize continuing sin in the life of a Jesus-follower.

The commonly used term "carnal Christian" is a carryover from the King James Version of the 1 Corinthians 3:1-3 passage. Sometimes, Jesus-followers argue that since there were carnal Christians in the church at Corinth, carnality in a Christian's life is normal.

To a degree, I agree with this argument. In context, the word "carnal" is used to describe new, immature Jesus-followers. Since new Jesus-followers don't instantly mature, there will always be some degree of carnality within the Christian community.

However, when this scripture passage is used to rationalize continuing sin as normal in the life of a Jesus-follower, I have to disagree. I believe that this goes far beyond what Paul was trying to communicate. There is no place in the Bible where continuing immaturity is described as normal. It's not true in physical life. Why would it be true in spiritual life?

I Timothy 1:12-15 Passage

This is still another scripture passage that is sometimes referenced to rationalize continuing sin in the life of a Jesus-follower.

> I thank him who has given me strength, Christ Jesus our Lord, because he judged me faithful, appointing me to his service, though formerly I was a blasphemer, persecutor, and insolent

opponent. But I received mercy because I had acted ignorantly in unbelief, and the grace of our Lord overflowed for me with the faith and love that are in Christ Jesus. The saying is trustworthy and deserving of full acceptance, that Christ Jesus came into the world to save sinners, of whom I am the foremost.

1Timothy 1:12-15

Jesus-followers, who use this passage as rationale for continuing sin, focus on "I am the foremost" statement in the passage that is referring to "sinners." Thus, they see Paul describing himself as the foremost of all sinners, and thereby rationalize their own condition as being normal.

However, in order to understand his statement, we need to consider the time in his life he was referring to. Was it during his regenerate life, as an apostle, or was it before his Damascus Road conversion as a religious Jew? To me, it seems obvious that this question is answered within the context of Paul describing his former life as a religious Jew who denied Jesus as the Messiah and persecuted his followers.

Within context, I don't believe Paul's description of himself as the "foremost of all sinners" can be rightly used to rationalize continuing sin in the lives of Jesus-followers.

CONCLUSIONS

In this chapter, I have discussed common misapplications of certain scripture passages that are sometimes used to rationalize continuing sin in the lives of Jesus-followers. I wrote the chapter because I believe these misapplications continue to have a significantly negative impact on how the Christian life is perceived and lived.

Based on the above scripture analysis, I don't believe Paul's life, *as an apostle*, was characterized by bondage to sin. Nor do I believe his life can, in any way, be used to rationalize continuing sin in the lives of Jesus-followers.

I believe the full scope of God's grace includes the provision to overcome sin's bondage. There will always be conflicts between desires of the flesh and desires of the Spirit. However, the scripture tells us that if we "walk by the Spirit," we "will not gratify the desires of the flesh." (Galatians 5:16) If we consistently do this, we will experience the "abundant life" Jesus came to give us. (John 10:10) If we don't, we continue to experience defeated lives, which is detrimental to us and God's Kingdom.

PERSONAL NOTE

My personal experience is compatible with the above conclusions. There was an extended period in my life, as a professing Christian, when I could identify with the sin bondage Paul describes in Romans 7. However, after God intervened in my life at age 37, I began a new life Paul describes in Romans 8. It's not that I never sin. It's just that sin in not an overwhelming, or seemingly insurmountable, issue in my life. When the Holy Spirit convicts me of sin, I quickly come to the realization that fellowship with my Father is more important than my sin, and I repent.

For me, this is a natural consequence of being "born of God." (1 John 3:9) It is what my "new self" (Ephesians 4:24) desires to do. This is not unique to me. I know and regularly associate with other Jesus-followers who fully understand and identify with my experience.

Chapter 17
Conceptual Terms

Although the theological viewpoints expressed in this chapter are consistent with the rest of the book, I realize they are somewhat contradictory to other (maybe the majority of) viewpoints within the evangelical community of which I am a part. Thus, my natural inclination is to leave the chapter out of the book. However, as best I can determine, the Lord will not let me do that. Therefore, if you choose to read the chapter, please know I write it as my side of a loving dialogue I would like to have with you. I am very much aware I could be wrong, but humbly submit it for your consideration.

BACKGROUND

During the past forty years of my spiritual pilgrimage, I have been continually exposed to two conceptual terms that are commonly used to explain certain aspects of Christian life. As we will learn in the following discussion, they are not directly translated biblical terms. They were coined by well-meaning theologians to help explain difficult biblical truths.

Although I could not personally relate to the theological viewpoint that these terms represented, I tolerated them and went on my merry way. However, in the past several years, based on observations and discussions with other Jesus-followers, I have come to see that these terms can have unintended consequences. They can be a major impediment to experiencing the abundant life Jesus came to give. Further,

I see them as so strongly entrenched in the evangelical Christian community, of which I am a part, that it is considered almost heretical to even question them. Thus, I see them as having a continuing negative impact on how the Christian life is perceived and lived.

Sin Nature

Sin Nature is a commonly used term that Jesus-followers are routinely exposed to in sermons, teachings and Christian media of various kinds. It was coined by theologians to describe human nature in a way that explains our well-recognized strong propensity to sin. However, based on interactions with large numbers of Jesus-followers during the past forty years, I believe this conceptualization of our nature can create a false perception of how the Christian life is to be lived. Please let me explain.

All Jesus-followers correctly understand that their spiritual standing with God is not based on their merit. It is entirely based upon what God has done for them through Jesus. Although they understand we are saved "by grace…through faith" (Ephesians 2:8), they also realize they still have a strong propensity to sin. Thus, it is easy to adopt Sin Nature as a term to explain the root cause of this propensity. However, is this viewpoint biblical?

A simple word search of today's most commonly used Bible versions quickly reveals that *the term "Sin Nature" is never used*. Based on this fact alone, I wonder how the term has gained such widespread usage.

Although none of the commonly used Bible versions use *Sin Nature*, two of the versions use a similar term, *Sinful*

Nature. The NLT uses this term twenty times, and the NIV uses it two times. Neither of these versions is strictly word-for-word (WFW) translations. In an attempt to achieve clarity, they sometimes use thought-for-thought (TFT) translations. It is also interesting to note that the earlier 1983 NIV used Sinful Nature similarly to today's NLT. However, when revised to the most recent 2011 edition, the NIV uses the term only two times. Based on this trend, it is reasonable to anticipate that any future revision of the NLT will similarly minimize use of the Sinful Nature term.

Now let's review what we have learned. So far, we've learned that Sin Nature is a commonly used conceptual term to describe human nature, but it is not a biblical term. Since we are biblical Jesus-followers, we need to determine if use of this non-biblical term can cause any problems.

To do this, we need to review what we learned earlier about human nature. In the Part 2 description of "The Biblical Human Being," we concluded that human nature is not *intrinsically* sinful! (If you have any questions about this conclusion, please review Chapter 4.)

Based on this conclusion, we can see a potential problem the Sin Nature term may cause. For me, and I believe the same is true for most people, Sin Nature strongly implies that sin is intrinsic to our basic human nature. If we see ourselves as *intrinsically* sinful, we have difficulty seeing that we can overcome sin. In other words, we tend to think it's impossible to go against our basic nature.

Also, we tend to see the whole of scripture through the lens of this viewpoint. When I talk to other Jesus-followers, this is what I sometimes find. As explained in the previous chapter, they use particular scripture passages (e.g., Romans 7:14-24) to rationalize their sin bondage as the normal status quo for the Christian life.

On the other hand, if we see ourselves as only having a propensity to sin, we can more readily see the possibility of overcoming it, especially when we consider divine influence. As those born of God (born again), *we have divine influence*. We have the indwelling Holy Spirit! The Bible clearly states, "…walk by the Spirit, and you will not gratify the desires of the flesh." (Galatians 5:16) *Therefore, to the degree that we walk by the Spirit, we can overcome sin!* We will not do this perfectly, but we can and should be continually moving toward that goal.

Imputed Righteousness

Imputed Righteousness (sometimes expressed as Positional Righteousness) is another commonly used term Jesus-followers are routinely exposed to. The term is based on a theological viewpoint that perfection is required for man to have a right relationship with Holy God. This viewpoint leads to the concept of man's sin being imputed to Jesus and Jesus' righteousness being imputed to man. This conceptualization is sometimes referred to as "The Great Exchange" (exchanging man's sin for Jesus' righteousness). Based on this viewpoint, Jesus' imputed righteousness is seen as the legal basis on which a person can have a right standing before God. Thus, the biblical references that state we are "justified by faith" are typically understood to mean that faith is the conduit through which we are justified by imputed righteousness.

This theological viewpoint can be very soothing to Jesus-followers who see themselves as having a sin nature that can't be overcome. For example, I sometimes hear them express attitudes like, "I'm just a poor old rotten sinner, and that's all I will ever be, but when God looks at me, he only sees the righteousness of Jesus." This attitude is the logical conclusion of believing that one has an intrinsic sin nature but also imputed righteousness. Such an attitude may sooth the conscience, but it can also numb it to the point that Jesus-followers are content to accept continuing sin bondage as the status quo for the Christian life.

As was the case for Sin Nature, it is interesting to note that *none of the commonly used Bible versions use the Imputed Righteousness term*. However, adherents of this theology cite scripture passages they see as implying the need for and reality of imputed righteousness. When I examine their arguments, it seems they always start with a conclusion and then find scripture passages that supposedly support their conclusion. Based on a careful examination of commonly cited scripture passages, I don't see any of them that *demand* an imputed righteousness interpretation.

Further, I believe the term leads to logical conundrums. Does God really put on some kind of rose-colored glasses when he looks at us? Does he not see us as we really are? Also, the Bible says, "All Scripture is breathed out by God and profitable for teaching, for reproof, for correction, and for training in *righteousness,* that the man of God may be complete, equipped for every good work." (2 Timothy 3:16-17, emphasis added) This is clearly referring to personal character and conduct, not some mystical imputed righteousness. If God only sees the righteousness of Jesus when he looks at us, what did the Apostle John mean when he said, "Whoever *practices* righteousness is righteous"? (1 John 3:7, emphasis added) My mind is not capable of the mental gymnastics necessary to solve such riddles.

SUMMARY

In this chapter, I have attempted to explain the etymology and common usage of two conceptual terms I believe can have unintended consequences. When the terms are combined, as they typically are, the consequences can be profound. For the past forty-plus years, I have seen this in the lives of many seemingly genuine Jesus-followers whom I have known and associated with. On one hand, because of a perceived intrinsic sin nature, they see themselves as unable to overcome sin. On the other hand, because of a perceived imputed righteousness, they are desensitized to the importance of living pure lives.

Because of potential unintended consequences, I believe the community of Jesus-followers should be very careful when using these or other extra-biblical conceptual terms. I don't see them as necessary to explain essential theological truths. The biblical terms "flesh" and "justified by faith" adequately describe human nature and how imperfect humans can have a right relationship with Holy God.

Chapter 18
Majoring in Minors

For decades, I have been an avid participant and observer of Christianity in the U.S. where I reside. During the past several years, I have contemplated how its evolved version compares to the biblical description of what it should be.

My conclusion is that we have largely deviated from biblical Christianity. Years ago, I heard a sermon entitled "Shifting Deck Chairs on the Titanic." For me, that title is an apt metaphor for my observations. As a result, I see us, as the body of Christ, largely "majoring in minors."

How did this happen, and what do we need to do to get back on track?

DIVERSIONS

I see three major diversions within the body of Christ that contributed to the current state of Christianity in the U.S.

Dilution of the Gospel Message

As described in Part 1, I believe that at some point before my generation came on scene, the gospel message in the U.S. began to get diluted, and my generation and subsequent ones have allowed it to continue. As a result, today's Christianity has largely lost its power to transform, overcome, and enable its adherents as compared to descriptions in the early church.

This realization was, at least partly, behind my motivation to write this book. It was an attempt to do my part in somehow righting the ship. In Parts 1 and 2, I attempted to at least stall and hopefully contribute to reversing the dilution trend. I can only hope and pray I was successful for some readers.

Obsessions With Certain Biblical Topics

Although any physical or mental obsession can divert us from fulfilling God's kingdom objectives, spiritual obsessions can also cause diversions.

Please note that I'm not talking about in-depth studies necessary to understand and explain difficult biblical topics as best we can. But when a particular topic becomes an obsession to the point that it's the primary focus of our spiritual life, we have diverted from our primary mandate as followers of Jesus.

Among various Christian sects within the U.S., these obsessions come in many "shapes and sizes." As examples, I will describe three that I have been particularly sensitized to during my forty plus as a follower of Jesus.

Creation

Starting early in my spiritual journey as a Jesus-follower in the 1970s, and continuing for a number of years, I was obsessed with attempting to resolve "apparent" conflicts between the biblical account of creation and modern science claims. Eventually, I adopted a scientific hypothesis that seemed to best resolve the apparent conflicts. However, as modern science evolved, my hypothesis became increasingly hard to rationalize.

Looking back, I now see my (and others) efforts in this regard as a diversion from Jesus' primary mandate to "go therefore and make disciples." (Matthew 28:18-20) Although current attempts to resolve the apparent conflicts are not as pervasive as they were during earlier times in U.S. history, I see them today as lingering obsessions for some Jesus-followers and thereby a continuing diversion from our primary mandate.

I also see the negative impact this obsession can potentially have on perceived credibility of the Christian faith. I was sensitized to this potential a few years ago when observing a gospel presentation in one of the South American countries. I had just completed a mission project in that country and was overnighting in an airport hotel prior to my return to the U.S. While relaxing in the hotel plaza, I met and began conversing with a couple who were involved in a different but similar mission project. During our conversation, it became obvious that a young Scandinavian woman, sitting nearby, was listening to us.

To make a long story short, the couple eventually began witnessing to the young woman. As part of their gospel presentation, they used the same scientific hypothesis I had previously adopted. As the young woman listened, it became obvious that, although she had very little knowledge of biblical Christianity, she was somewhat versed in modern science and obviously wasn't "buying" what the couple was selling. As I listened, I surprisingly found myself not buying it either. In fact, I realized the couple's arguments were having an opposite affect than intended. They were unintentionally creating doubt about the Bible's credibility.

Since then, I have been sensitized to how modern science should be addressed during gospel presentations. Generally, I think we should focus on the gospel message of the Bible and avoid peripheral subjects as much as possible. If forced into scientific discourse, we should stand firm on the biblical assertion that God created everything we know, but not be dogmatic about the process he used to do it. I have found that apologetics-type discussions, along the lines described in Appendix 3, to be *satisfactorily responsive and non-offensive* to most gospel presentation recipients. For those readers who desire to be more proficient in sharing the gospel, I recommend you study the appendix or other apologetic arguments to the point where you can confidently rationalize the Bible's *supernatural* creation claims.

End Times Eschatology

In addition to other pastimes, I am an amateur musician who performs at "jam" sessions within the area surrounding where my wife and I reside. At one of these jams, we were made aware of an upcoming "revival meeting" planned for a small church in a typical rural Texas town where my wife was born and close to where we were both raised.

Since regular "revival meetings" were part of our heritage, and we were very familiar with where this one was being held, we agreed it would be a fun trip down memory lane to attend the meeting.

At this point, I need to describe the revival meetings that flourished throughout the U.S. during our childhood and continued through our early adulthood. In essence, they were events (typically about one-week in duration) arranged by local churches and designed as evangelistic outreaches to the community in which the church resided. Typically, well-known musicians and a speaker were advertised through local media and word of mouth to attract attention and hopefully gain increased attendance. Each night of the meeting, an evangelistic gospel message was presented and an invitation given to those interested in becoming "Christians."

With our background, this is the type of meeting my wife and I were anticipating when we attended the last night of the revival. As anticipated, there was "special" music and a "well-known" speaker. However, the meeting was not evangelistic in any sense of the word. The speaker presented a focused and dramatically forceful message about End Times Eschatology of a particular persuasion. Hence, the gospel wasn't explained and an expected salvation invitation wasn't appropriate or given.

As I pondered this and other similar experiences of recent years, I became highly sensitized to how must time and resources the body of Christ is expending to understand and promote various eschatology viewpoints. Is this really consistent with Jesus' primary mandate to his followers? We certainly need to study God's Word and understand that a key aspect of our common faith is Jesus' second coming to planet Earth, but is the exact process of how he does it really that important? Personally, I think not! Wouldn't it be better, as good stewards of God's resources, to spend them on Jesus' clearly stated primary mandate to go unto the whole world to "make disciples?"

Spiritual Gifts

Here I have to be very careful. I don't want to disparage anyone's gifting or imply that some are more important than others. They are all essential for a healthy functioning body of Christ. Each one has been designed and assigned by God to work together in accomplishing his kingdom objectives. However, when an obsession with any one of them causes us to deviate from God's intended purpose, they too can be, effectively, "majoring in minors."

As an example, several years ago as a participant on a mission trip to Cuba, I found myself as a roommate with a very flamboyant "drugstore cowboy" from West Texas. The mission team's objective was purely evangelism. However, the "cowboy" immediately started telling everyone he came in contact with about the many physical healings God had used him to perform, including, as I remember, thirty-nine resurrections from the dead.

As a result, he was the center of attraction wherever he went and "reportedly" performed several physical healings during the mission trip. One evening before bedtime, after listening to his many stories, I told him that if I somehow died in his presence, "Please don't attempt to resurrect me from the dead." This may have come across as a "put-down," but I meant what I said. Why would I want to die twice? Maybe if I was a non-Christian and needed more time to come to know God, or if, as a Jesus-follower, God had some unknown purpose for my life, a resurrection would make sense. But just to spend more time on planet Earth when I could be in God's eternal presence was not an attractive proposition to me. It wasn't at the time and still isn't!

I have no doubt God can and does heal today, including possible resurrections from the dead. But if we are not careful, obsession with physical healing can effectively be "missing the forest for the trees" and thereby be a diversion from our primary mandate to "make disciples."

I further believe the same rationale can be applied to all the spiritual gifts listed in 1 Corinthians 12. The apostle Paul made it clear that all of them are important within the body of Christ, but they should not be used obsessively as "spiritual badges" to promote self-edification. In contrast, they should only be used when clearly led by the Holy Spirit to edify the body of Christ and thus further God's kingdom objectives. Otherwise, they can become major distractions from our primary mandate to make disciples.

Divergence From the Gospel Mandate

In U.S. churches today, I have seen an increasing trend to prioritize social welfare type projects. These efforts are typically designed to make physical life a little better for needy people. The intentions are good, and some people are undoubtedly helped through desperate situations. However, I believe *some* of these efforts have caused us to divert from our primary gospel mandate.

Yes, the New Testament certainly commands that we are to "love your neighbor as yourself." (Mark 12:31) In Jesus' parable of the "Good Samaritan," we learn that our neighbor is *anyone* we come across in life who needs our help.

It's easier to follow the commandment for those we already know and love but harder for those we don't know. However, for those we don't know, it helps to keep in mind that they may already be a brother or sister in Christ who has desperate needs God desires to meet through us. Or if they aren't already a brother or sister in Christ, maybe our act of kindness will be the impetus that God uses to bring them into his family.

Throughout the New Testament, we see various ways Jesus and his early followers fulfilled the commandment to love their neighbors regardless of established relationships with them. These records serve as examples for us. This is all good and right!

However, we don't see New Testament examples of large-scale efforts to solve society's ills. As we learned earlier in this book, all problems in the world can ultimately be traced to human sin. The gospel addresses the spiritual root cause of problems rather than just the physical symptoms. When the root is healthy, the tree flourishes. This is why biblical Christianity always has a positive impact on societies.

When we focus on symptoms, rather than the root, we deviate from our God-given mandate. In effect, the social efforts can become a substitute for sharing the gospel. In the extreme, they can even *become the gospel* in some people's minds.

Also, through our good intentions and zeal to help people have better lives, we may create bigger problems. For example, where are people most resistant to the gospel? Is it not in societies where affluence and self-sufficiency are most prominent? If we fix people's symptoms, but not the root cause, have we not contributed to a possible hardening of their hearts toward the gospel? In addition, there is the question of stewardship. If we spend most of our God-given resources on fixing social ills, have we not decreased our ability to fulfill our primary mandate to make disciples?

Please understand that I am not talking about social efforts used as platforms to share the gospel. As I write this book, my wife (with me as her chief "roadie") functions as leader for our church's efforts to support the Samaritan's Purse Operation Christmas Child (OCC) project. This ministry recruits volunteer individuals and people groups to purchase and pack Christmas shoe boxes with toys and other personal items, such as clothing and hygiene items, for underprivileged children throughout the world. Some of these children have never received a present of any kind, so just the present in itself is a practical, tangible way to "love your neighbor as yourself." However, when the children receive the present, they are also given the opportunity to participate in a 12-week Bible study. If they complete the study and make a decision to become a follower of Jesus, they are given a personal Bible in their own language, which in many parts of the world is a highly treasured gift, to aid their spiritual growth.

Thus, OCC and many other similar ministries are completely in line with our primary objectives to make disciples. I realize some people may see these kinds of efforts as manipulative. My only answer is that we must stay true to our biblical mandate. In my mind, it is never inappropriate to share the gospel, if we do it in a loving and sensitive way.

REFOCUSING

All genuine Jesus-followers agree that our common, ultimate objective is to "make disciples" as commanded by Jesus (Matthew 28:19). And they understand that after his resurrection, this mandate was further amplified when he said, "But you will receive power when the Holy Spirit has come upon you, and you will be my witnesses in Jerusalem and in all Judea and Samaria, and to the end of the earth." (Acts 1:8)

Yet, I don't see a passion in most Jesus-followers to accomplish his mandate. They seem content to just live relatively moral lifestyles and be involved in church life. If they are really spiritual, they may obsess over some particular non-evangelistic related biblical topic or get involved in some type of social help type ministry as described earlier in the chapter. They will readily give lip service to the need for evangelism, but typically see it as someone else's calling and ministry. Sometimes, they even see evangelism as an embarrassing intrusion into other people's worldview and, by word or deed, discourage or impede (probably unintentionally) evangelistic efforts.

As members of the Body of Christ, we need to return to first principles. In order to do this, we need to see God's creation through his eyes and join in what he is doing. So, how do we do this?

First, we need to understand that when God looks at his creation, he sees the whole world. God cares about *all* people and does not desire that "any should perish." (2 Peter 3:9) He is continually working throughout the world to make himself known and to draw people to himself. As a result, there are always fields "white for harvest" (John 4:35) somewhere in the world. Today, this the case for Central and South America, many African countries, many of the islands of the world, parts of Asia, and probably many other areas I don't personally know about.

Although there are some notable exceptions, this is generally not the current case for North America, Europe, and other Western cultures. This certainly doesn't mean we shouldn't evangelize in these places. But every good fisherman knows that 90% of fish are caught in 10% of the lake. Therefore, as wise stewards of God's resources, I believe we need to continually evaluate how and where we are fishing.

Second, we need to understand that in all life endeavors, vision and focus are key to success! Jesus' vision was clearly focused on making disciples. As his followers, we need to have the same mindset. This will not be easy for the diverse groups of people with different backgrounds and giftings that comprise U.S. churches. It will require strong leadership, clear and consistent teaching, undivided commitment, and unyielding perseverance.

If we maintain our focus on first principles, as described above, we will be fulfilling God's mandate for all Jesus-followers. As a result, we will be able to say with Jesus, "*My food* is to do the will of him (my Father) who sent me and to accomplish his work." (John 4:34, parentheses added) And we will experience the joy of "oneness" within the Body of Christ that we desire and that Jesus prayed for us to have. (John 17)

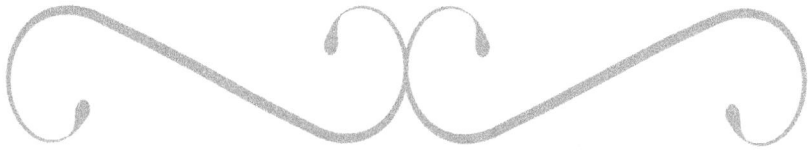

Part 5

Appendices

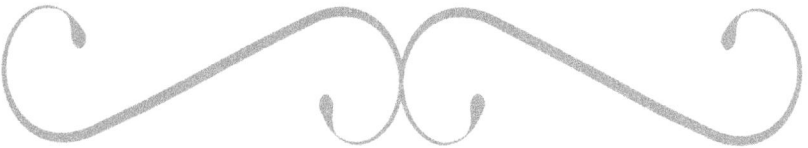

Appendix 1
My Spiritual Journey

As I reflect on my life, it seems that everything has been orchestrated. It seems I was created for the specific purpose I am now performing within the kingdom of God. I realize this may be a controversial assessment, but doesn't God's Word state, "And we know that for those who love God all things work together for good, for those who are called according to his purpose?" (Romans 8:28)

You may respond, "But you didn't always love God," which is true. But what if an omniscient (all-knowing) God had a plan for my life before the foundation of the world and knew I would one day come to love him? Then, it makes sense he would orchestrate my life to accomplish his objective. I am not pushing this viewpoint, but I think it's a distinct possibility, and I don't know where it conflicts with scripture.

So let me tell my story, and you decide if this viewpoint has any merit.

PERSONAL ENCOUNTER WITH GOD

I first heard about God and his plan of salvation as a young boy at a small rural church my family attended. When I was 12 years old, in response to a church service invitation, I publicly "accepted Jesus as my Savior" and was later baptized in a local creek. From that time, I cannot remember having any serious doubts about God or what the Bible taught. I believed I was a Christian and would go to Heaven when I died.

However, even though I intellectually believed, I did not have any real comprehension of what it meant to have a relationship with God or to be a follower of Jesus. I do remember having vague feelings from time to time that God had a plan for my life but was unwilling to make the commitment to find out what God's plan was or to pursue it.

During what I call my spiritual wandering years, which lasted from age 12 to 37, I continued to believe in God and Jesus. However, if you observed my lifestyle during that time span, it wouldn't have been apparent. Along the way, I spent time in the Marine Corps, married my childhood sweetheart, got an electrical engineering degree, fathered three children, and engaged in what turned out to be a highly successful career. However, my life during those years was all about me. I was the center of my universe. My life consisted of work, partying, outdoor sports, and involvement in a bluegrass music group. I had very little quality time for my wife and children. I had a few friends, but our interests were not always God-honoring. I sporadically took my family to church, but my spiritual life was in shambles and essentially nonexistent.

Also, during this time span, some things happened that got my serious attention. First, my father and father-in-law, who was also my good friend, both died unexpectedly at an early age. Second, I began to experience some health issues of the same type that caused my father's death. And third, although I was on a fast-track career path, I began to experience an emptiness and lack of purpose in life. This was accentuated by a heavy sense of guilt in knowing I had not lived the life God planned for me. Thus, I became very angry at life in general and with myself particularly. I had done all society told me to do, but it wasn't enough. And when I looked at myself in a mirror, I didn't like the person I saw.

This accumulation of circumstances, and my reaction to them, led me to think that maybe my problems had a spiritual root. As a result, I started attending a small church where I saw people with new eyes. I saw that people were there for a variety of reasons. Some were there because of family traditions. Some because of spousal demands or because they wanted their children to be there. And some were there purely for social interaction. However, I also saw some whose lives reflected what they professed to believe. They were not perfect, but it was obvious they were experiencing a meaningful relationship with God that I wasn't.

As a result, I began to seriously read the Bible. In a way I can't fully explain, the Bible became alive to me. It wasn't just some stories about ancient people. It had real application to everyday life situations. Sometimes, as I read futuristic prophecies, it was almost like reading about world events in the daily newspaper. I began to see Jesus as a real person, not just part of an intellectual spiritual viewpoint. He became a person I admired and who was worthy of my love and devotion. He became a person I wanted to follow!

Finally, at age 37, all my life experiences culminated in a personal encounter with God. I remember sitting by my kitchen table confessing to God how I had messed up my life and pleading for forgiveness. I don't remember everything I said that day, but I do remember telling God something to the effect of, "Whatever it means and wherever it takes me, I want to be a follower of Jesus for the rest of my life."

That day my life was dramatically transformed. I was immediately set free from several sin strongholds I had struggled with for years. As I fed my new spiritual appetite from the Bible and all kinds of spiritual media, I developed an intense desire to fulfil the purpose I had been created for.

GOD'S CALLING

Shortly after that experience, I had another encounter with God. My wife and I, along with another couple, attended a weekend Christian conference at a retreat center in south Texas a few hours from the place where we lived. On the way, my friend, Bob, casually asked me a question I had never considered, "Ed, if you could only do one thing for the rest of your life, what would it be?"

That question somehow penetrated the deepest part of my being. I don't even remember what the weekend conference was about. My thoughts that weekend were consumed by the question Bob had asked, but I couldn't come up with a satisfying answer!

On the trip back home, Bob interrupted my thoughts with, "Well Ed, what's the answer to my question?"

Upon reflection, I don't think Bob planned what he was doing. I think the Holy Spirit was using him to speak directly to me.

As I contemplated his question, an unexpected answer was birthed somewhere deep in my innermost being. I replied, "Bob, if I could only do one thing for the rest of my life, it would be to tell people about Jesus in a simple way they could understand!"

RECEIVING GOD'S CALL

A third encounter with God happened at the local church I was attending. My church was participating in a new evangelistic program sponsored by the Southern Baptist Convention. The program was centered on wearing a small lapel pin for 30 days entitled "Living Proof." Hopefully, someone's curiosity about the pin would open the door for a spiritual conversation that could potentially lead to their salvation.

One Sunday evening, our pastor explained the program and invited members of the congregation to make a commitment to wear the pin for the 30-day period. I felt led to do this but was experiencing the most intense spiritual struggle of my life. Finally, realizing it was now or never, I mustered every ounce of my courage and walked forward to make my formal commitment.

The next Monday morning presented another major crisis. When I stepped out of my car to enter my workplace, wearing the pin, I was literally sweating with anxiety. I didn't want to be different; I just wanted to fit in. But I knew that wearing the pin would forever change the way people looked at me.

As I sat at my desk that day (or maybe a few days later – I don't remember for certain), one of the higher-ups in the company entered my office to talk to me. As he sat across the desk from me, I don't know if he saw the pin, but that possibility was all I could think about. Again, I experienced severe anxiety, approaching panic-attack level.

Today, the whole Living Proof experience seems almost trivial, but at the time it was the most traumatic spiritual step

I had taken. As a result, I fully understand the significance of Jesus' statement, "And I tell you, everyone who acknowledges me before men, the Son of Man also will acknowledge before the angels of God." (Luke 12:8) In a small but significant way, I had done this!

LIVING FORWARD

Looking back, I count the above encounters as the three most important milestones of my spiritual journey.

- Beginning to Follow Jesus as Lord.
- Learning God's Purpose for my Life.
- Taking a First Step toward Fulfilling God's Purpose for my Life.

These three milestones that I believe were very much God-orchestrated led to who I am today and what God has accomplished through me.

As stated in the Introduction, during the past forty-plus years, I have fulfilled my calling (gifting) within the body of Christ as a non-vocational evangelist. In this capacity I have seen thousands of people, in many countries of the world, come to a saving relationship with the Lord Jesus Christ. Considering my introverted personality and deficient social skills, I realize there is no rational explanation for these results apart from God's orchestration and gracious enabling!

Appendix 2
The Bible as a Credible Roadmap

In my role as an evangelist, I encounter many people who struggle with the Bible's credibility. They typically struggle with questions like, "Isn't the Bible just ancient writings by people who were much less knowledgeable than we are today," or "Isn't it just a collection of myths propagated by unsophisticated and superstitious people," or "How can its supernatural claims be real?"

This Appendix will examine the Bible as a credible roadmap for a spiritual journey that provides purpose and meaning in this life and hope for eternity.

CREDIBILITY OF THE BIBLE

Regardless of how persuasive my arguments are, I realize I will not be able to convince you that the Bible is credible. Only God can do that! However, for God to convince you, you must be open to the possibility of its truth. For those not open, the Bible says they "suppress the truth." (Romans 1:18) If that is what you have done to this point, why? Were you exposed to some media or listened to someone you considered authoritative? Do you really want to base your current life and eternal existence on someone else's opinion? Wouldn't it be better to at least consider the possibility that there is a personal being, called God, who has revealed himself in the Bible? And that this God loves you and put you here on planet Earth as part of his creation plan? And that his plan includes both meaning and purpose during this life and for all eternity?

If you are truly open, please consider the following arguments for the Bible's credibility.

The Bible's History

Scholars tell us the Bible was written over a period of about 1500 years, from about 1400 BC to 100 AD. It is composed of thirty-nine books in the Old Testament and twenty-seven books in the New Testament. The Old Testament was originally written in Hebrew and the New Testament in Greek and Aramaic. There is a time gap of about 400 years between the two Testaments.

Scholars also tell us that the books of the Old and New Testaments were written by about forty authors with diverse backgrounds. They represented a variety of social and geographical influences. In addition, the canonization processes for both Testaments were very complex. They were the products of Jewish rabbis for the Old Testament and Christian leaders for the New Testament. Because of their commitment to God's truth, it took extended periods of time for them to reach broad consensus. In these respects, the Bible is unique among all ancient books.

Theologians describe the authorship and canonization processes as "God inspired." This basically means that God guided human circumstances and thoughts to provide *his message* to humankind. Thus, it is called the "Word of God!"

Although there were earlier translations to other languages, the first English translation of the Bible was the King James Version, first published in 1611 AD. Today we benefit from many English versions, compiled by teams of well-credentialed scholars, who used different translation approaches such as word-for-word, thought-for-thought, paraphrase, and combinations thereof. Although sometimes expressed in different words, there is no divergence of major theological doctrines among these versions. Thus, we can conclude that the Bible's accuracy has been vetted by well-credentialed scholars more than any other book ever written. This fact alone should cause truth seekers to seriously consider its credibility.

The Bible's Message

Despite its diverse and complex history, the Bible provides comprehensive answers to our deepest questions. It describes how *one* omnipotent, omniscient, and omnipresent God, who is perfectly righteous and just in all that he does, created the cosmos (all that we know) from *nothing*. It further describes humanity as the pinnacle of his creation and explains:

- How We Came into Existence
- Why We Exist
- The Reason for Our Problems
- The Solution for Our Problems
- Our Eternal Destiny

After more than forty years of intensive study, like millions of others throughout the ages, I have found the biblical descriptions of our being to be both rational and in agreement with experience. Who but our Creator could provide such descriptions?

The Bible's Self-authentication

Its self-authentication is probably the strongest argument for the Bible's credibility. Many scholars, eminently more qualified than I, have addressed this subject in detail. In this book, I will highlight only a few of the more obvious examples of its self-authentication.

Historical Records

The Bible contains detailed, verifiable historical records, including:

- The genealogy of modern humanity from its origin to Jesus.
- The early development and geological dispersion of modern humanity people groups.
- The identity and descriptions of relevant, ancient nations/kingdoms/empires from the time of Abraham until the beginning of Christianity (~ 2000 years).
- The development of Christianity during the 1st century AD.

Although scholars have found some spelling and name variations in early hand-copied manuscripts, no major historical discrepancies have ever been verified. This is after many decades of modern, sometimes critical, research. In fact, each new verifiable (not just some hypothesis based on meager evidence) archeological discovery has only increased our confidence in the Bible's credibility.

Fulfilled Prophesies

The Old Testament of the Bible contains some 200

prophecies of a coming Messiah that were written hundreds of years before the New Testament. It has been mathematically shown that the probability of these prophecies being fulfilled by chance is, for all practical purposes, statistically impossible. Yet Jesus fulfilled every one of them. The only rational conclusion is that Jesus is the prophesied Messiah!

In addition, The Bible contains many other fulfilled promises and prophecies, including:

- Many Old Testament promises to Abraham and his descendants about "The Promised Land."
- Many Old Testament prophecies concerning the Israelite people and surrounding nations, kingdoms, and empires.
- New Testament prophecies by Jesus about his forthcoming betrayal/death/resurrection, the coming of the Holy Spirit, the destruction of the Jewish temple, and the perpetual persecution of his followers.

The fulfillment of these promises and prophecies provides additional credence to the already strong evidence for the Bible's credibility.

Eyewitness Accounts

The Bible contains multiple eyewitness accounts of Jesus' earthly ministry. These witnesses were close followers of Jesus during his three-year earthly ministry. Their eyewitness accounts, recorded in the New Testament, include his:

- Supernatural miracles that had no explanation apart from divine origin.

- Teachings that far exceed human wisdom.
- Crucifixion, burial, and empty tomb.
- Multiple resurrected body appearances during a forty-day period.
- Ascension into heaven.

Based on such compelling evidence, how could these eyewitnesses not believe Jesus was who he said? And, if we were jurors in a present-day court of law, would we not believe the testimonies of such eyewitnesses? So again, we see additional strong evidence of the Bible's credibility.

The Bible's Survival

Many critics, over thousands of years, have tried to dismiss the Bible's credibility, and some societies even tried to keep it from being available to its people.

Others have charged that Christians are just ignorant or superstitious people. However, can this really be a valid charge in the face of clear evidence that many of the world's most brilliant philosophical and scientific minds have been Christians?

Others have attempted to discredit the Bible as being full of errors and contradictions. However, with the aid of continuing linguistic studies and archeological discoveries, biblical scholars have largely discounted these charges. There is broad consensus among biblical scholars that no major biblical doctrine departs from the original manuscripts and that any unexplained scribal errors or contradiction are inconsequential to the Bible's overall message.

Still others have tried to discredit the Bible based on

scientific evidence. However, as science progresses, it's becoming increasingly clear that there is no *natural* explanation for the existence of the cosmos, which is consistent with biblical claims. Although modern science doesn't help us understand who God is, it does provide a solid basis to philosophically argue for his existence. (If you are interested in my versions of these arguments, please turn to Appendix 3.)

More recently, some critics have attacked the Bible's claim of absolute truth. They do this by philosophically dismissing the existence of such truth. However, if we are intellectually honest, we soon realize we do not have the ability to dismiss its existence. In reality, we can only have opinions that may or may not be true. These opinions are generally the product of our upbringing, our culture, or just something we want to believe. If truth exists, it must be revealed to us from outside our being. Why is it unreasonable to conclude that God, as creator of all things, is the only viable source of absolute truth and that this truth has been revealed in the Bible?

While its critics come and go, the Bible continues to live as the Word of God for multitudes of people of diverse races and cultures throughout the world. And many of these people, as did the early disciples, continue to believe the truth of the Bible to the point of being martyred for their faith.

Thus, the Bible's survivability, in the face of relentless and sometimes vicious criticism, lends additional evidence of its credibility.

PERSONAL NOTE

I fully realize my brief arguments have not proved that the Bible is the inspired Word of God and therefore, the only source of absolute truth. However, if I put all evidence (postulated by others) that it's not true in one pile and the above evidence that it's true in another pile, the latter pile is much larger. *After studying the Bible for more than forty years, I cannot point to a single, verifiable untruth.*

Thus, my belief is the Bible is not based on blind faith, as some people suppose. It is based on carefully weighed evidence. Therefore, I have made a choice to accept the Bible as my ship for sailing life. I do this by faith, believing it is the most logical and beneficial choice I can make.

What if my choice is right and the Bible is the revelation of a loving God to his creation? What if it is God breathed and the only source of absolute truth? Aren't these possibilities worth serious consideration? If you haven't already, I sincerely hope and pray you will. Your fulfillment in life and eternal destiny rests on your decision!

Appendix 3
Philosophical Arguments
for God's Existence

As a non-vocational evangelist, during my career and since, I have had the opportunity to interact with thousands of people in many diverse cultures and life situations. When asked, a very high percentage of people whom I have talked to say they believe in God. Even those who have little knowledge or distorted views of God nevertheless say they believe. My objective in this appendix is to successfully argue that belief in a supernatural being, called God, is not irrational.

There is nothing new in my arguments. They are well known by Christian apologists. My simplified versions of the arguments draw from various articles, books, and conferences I have been exposed to over the years.

THE ARGUMENTS

As a starting point, we need to understand that the existence of God can neither be proved nor disproved. Many on both sides of the argument have tried, but all have failed.

This naturally leads to the question, "If we can't prove or disprove God's existence, why not just give up and be satisfied with an agnostic position?" I, along with multitudes of rational people throughout human history, have concluded that *the risk is too high*! If I simply ignore this risk, am I not like the proverbial ostrich that sticks its head in the sand?

We make many decisions throughout life without absolute proof they are right – such as getting married, having children, choosing work professions, making major purchases or financial investments, or seeing particular doctors. We make these decisions by rationally considering alternatives and choosing our path based on the best available evidence. Is not a decision that could determine our eternal destiny much more important than any of these temporal decisions?

Therefore, as rational human beings, let's consider some basic arguments for God's existence.

Arguments From Science

To proceed with this argument, we need to understand three generally accepted tenets of modern science.

- The cosmos is defined by time, space, and matter/energy.
- The cosmos had a beginning.
- Everything that exists in the cosmos has a cause.

Since the cosmos is defined by natural properties that had a beginning, it is rational to conclude that before its beginning, the properties did not exist. In other words, before the cosmos's beginning, ***nothing natural existed***! This may be hard to imagine, especially for time and space, but there is no verifiable evidence to dispute this rationale.

With this background, let's now examine possible causes for the cosmos' existence. From a philosophical viewpoint, possibilities fall within two categories - ***Natural*** (within the purview of modern science), or *Supernatural* (beyond natural).

Based on the modern science tenets stated above, arguments for a natural cause quickly result in logical conundrums.

1. Either a "seed cause" always existed and therefore had no beginning.
2. Or a seed cause originated from nothing and therefore had no cause.

Most espousers of a natural cause ignore these conundrums. They simply start with the assumption that something must have existed to initiate evolutionary processes. However, since they offer no scientific basis for this assumption, their argument lacks credibility.

The argument for a supernatural cause has a similar conundrum. What was the source (the cause) of the supernatural cause? However, it can be argued that a supernatural cause, by definition, would not be subject to tenets of modern science that require a cause.

Arguments From Design

It is obvious, even to casual observers, that the cosmos is incomprehensibly complex. This complexity exists at both microscopic and macroscopic levels.

At the microscopic level, how can we comprehend living cells that can be described as being more complex than present day factories or large cities? And there are more of these cells in the human body (up to 100 trillion by some estimates) than there are trees on the planet Earth.

Then, at the macroscopic level, how can we comprehend billions of galaxies with the largest containing more than a trillion stars? Or a galaxy that is 13.3 billion light years (a light year is 5.8 trillion miles) from planet Earth?

In addition to complexity, it is a well-accepted fact that the physical properties of planet Earth are finely tuned for human life. Even minute changes in these properties (such as distance from the sun, spin rate, and gravitational forces) would eliminate the possibility of human life as we know it.

Both complexity and fine tuning for a specific purpose are strong arguments for design. And design implies a designer! A designer implies a mind. And a mind implies a being of some type!

So now, in collaboration with the previous section, we have rationalized the possibility of an eternal, supernatural (spirit) being who designed and created the cosmos.

Arguments From Morality

In my interactions with people as an evangelist, I have found one thing in common. Except for cases of psychological abnormality, all people have an internal sense of right and wrong. Further, they sense all people should be held accountable for wrongs they have done!

Where did this moral sense come from? Some say it is the natural product of survival instincts, social necessities, and cultural leanings. To a degree, I agree with this assessment. I have witnessed how family environments and cultural influences (e.g., the entertainment industry) can greatly affect people's moral compass.

However, it is not obvious that these factors alone

adequately explain the universal sense of right, wrong, and accountability I have observed. It seems more rational that basic moral senses are somehow "wired" into the core of our being!

Since we obviously don't have the ability to wire ourselves, it is rational to conclude that our wiring must have originated from an external source. If we concede the possibility of a supernatural creator being, as rationalized in the previous two sections, why would this being not be the source of our wiring?

So again, our rationale points toward the existence of a supernatural, creator being whom we can call God.

Arguments From History

It is a well-attested historical and archeological fact that beliefs in the supernatural have played a major role in the development of all societies. These beliefs express themselves in the many religions that proliferate archeological and historical records.

Some argue that these religions are the superstitious product of fear. They argue that people generally fear the unknowns of life, particularly death, and therefore develop coping mechanisms for these fears. Thus, some have described religions as "crutches" to help "weaker" people get through life.

There may be some truth in this rationale for some people and some religions. However, there is another rationale I think better explains the proliferation of various religions throughout history.

In previous sections, we have rationalized the existence

of a supernatural creator being whom we called God. Suppose that, in addition to a moral compass described in the previous section, the knowledge of this God's existence was "wired" into our core being. Further, suppose that he was in intimate contact with the first-created man and woman. In this scenario, we have the basis for *a first and true religion*!

Now suppose that, as humankind multiplied and spread to different areas of the Earth, they formed tribes with unique cultural identities. They would initially retain memories of the *one true God*, but if they somehow became estranged from him, their memories over time would naturally fade.

However, they would still be wired with a general knowledge of God's existence. Therefore, they would naturally devise diverse, new concepts of God based on their personal cultural leanings. Thus, we would have the proliferation of various religions throughout history.

LIMITATIONS OF ARGUMENTS

In this appendix, I have philosophically argued, hopefully successfully, that belief in an eternal, supernatural being who we can call God is not irrational. As an evangelist, I have interacted with many people who philosophically agree with this conclusion. They readily agree that some type of "higher power" must exist.

However, although philosophy can point us toward God, it can't explain his attributes or his plan for humanity. We must look for other sources to answer these questions. Hopefully, the previous parts of the book answered questions you may have.

"And now I commend you to God and to the word of his grace, which is able to build you up and to give you the inheritance among all those who are sanctified."
~Acts 20:32

Bibliography

Creative Bible Study. n.d. "The Charles Blondin Story." *Creative Bible Study.* Accessed October 11, 2020. https://www.creativebiblestudy.com/Blondin-story.html.

Smith, Thayer and. 1999. "Greek Lexicon entry for Baptizo." *Bible Study Tools.* Accessed October 12, 2020. https://www.biblestudytools.com/lexicons/greek/nas/baptizo.html.

—. 1999. "Greek Lexicon entry for Kurios." *Bible Study Tools.* Accessed October 11, 2020. https://www.biblestudytools.com/lexicons/greek/nas/kurios.html.

—. 1999. "Greek Lexicon entry for Melanoia." *Bible Study Tools.* Accessed October 11, 2020. https://www.biblestudytools.com/lexicons/greek/nas/metanoia.html.

—. 1999. "Greek Lexicon entry for Sarx." *Bible Study Tools.* Accessed October 11, 2020. https://www.biblestudytools.com/lexicons/greek/nas/sarx.html.

About the Author

Edwin (Ed) Dittrich is a graduate of the University of Texas with a degree in electrical engineering. Until retirement at age 70, Ed was employed as a full-time electronic design/system engineer, first with NASA during the transition period between Gemini and Apollo missions, and later with two of the major defense contractors in the U.S. In this capacity, he led teams of technical experts to propose and develop some of the most sophisticated U.S. defense systems in use today. He had the privilege of knowing and working alongside a number of the brightest and most highly trained scientists and engineers in the world, and found this career to be both productive and fulfilling.

About nine years into his career, when he was 37 years old, he had an encounter with God that completely changed the focus of his life. As a result, in parallel with his career, he functioned as a non-vocational Christian evangelist when and wherever he had the opportunity. In this capacity, he initiated or participated in many fruitful evangelistic projects, both in the U.S. and internationally.

He is also an amateur country and bluegrass gospel musician who performs at various venues near his home. These venues are typically comprised of fellow musicians and audiences from a wide variety of spiritual backgrounds. He uses these opportunities to proclaim the gospel (the good news of Jesus) by singing and playing theologically sound Christian songs popularized by well-known country and bluegrass musicians.

Ed currently lives with his wife of over sixty years in

North Central Texas. He continues to be actively involved in various local and international evangelistic mission projects.

Contact Ed by email at eldittrich@charter.net.